Addingham in World War Two

Richard Thackrah & Beryl Falkingham

Edited by Don Barrett

First published 2017 by Addingham Civic Society
c/o The Old School, Main Street Addingham LS29 0NG Email:
info@addinghamcivicsociety.co.uk

Copyright © 2017
Beryl Falkingham & Richard Thackrah
All rights reserved.
ISBN: 1535597119
ISBN-13: 978-1535597111

DEDICATION

Dedicated to all those Addingham men and women who contributed to the war effort but particularly to the sixteen men from the village who died in the 1939-45 conflict

Addingham in World War Two

CONTENTS

	Acknowledgments	i
	Introduction	1
1	The Wartime Village	9
2	Local Press Reports	19
3	Addingham men who fell	71
4	More wartime stories	97
5	Air Crashes around Addingham	101
6	In Memoriam	107

ACKNOWLEDGMENTS

Sincere thanks to the many people who have helped or contributed to this book by supplying information by word of mouth, photographs, newspaper items or military records etc.

Special thanks are given to The Reverend Andrew Tawn, Rector of St Peter's Church from 1998 to 2012 and now Director of Clergy Development in the Leeds Diocese. In his Remembrance Service in 2010 he asked parishioners for their memories of World War Two, including details about some of the men named on the village war memorial. He obtained a certain amount of feedback and, also, information from a few people who had lost relatives during the war. However, to complete these details, more information was needed and it has been a privilege to continue with this after Andrew left the village. Grateful thanks are due to the relatives of men named on the War Memorial: Elizabeth Cooke, Kathleen Lister, Bessie Lovell, Jack Stapleton and Pauline Wild. The following local residents also provided invaluable information: Phyllis Robinson, Mary Readshaw, Margaret Holmes, George Kettlewell, Brenda Crooks and Eleanor Houston. Thanks also to Newsquest (North East) Ltd. for allowing full utilisation of the archives of the Ilkley Gazette at their former office in Ilkley, to various editors, particularly George Hinton, and other journalists; North Yorkshire Library staff in Skipton for allowing full access to the Craven Herald archives on microfiche; The Brotherton Library at Leeds University and Grantham Public Library in Lincolnshire; the authors of the Canadian Air Force Book of Remembrance; the website *ancestry.com.uk*; the Army's Roll of Honour 1939-1945 (database on-line); the National Archives War Office Roll of Honour and the Commonwealth War Graves Commission (CWGC) on-line sites, which all yielded much valuable information.

Gemma Croft spent many hours word processing, in a very professional way, the sections written by Richard Thackrah. Beryl Falkingham is very grateful to her husband Roy, as well as to Richard, for help with the research. Jonathan White has done excellent work in proofreading and checking, and thanks to Ken Birch for his excellent cartoons.

Last, but certainly not least, many thanks to Don Barrett for his expertise in formatting, editing and arranging publication by the Addingham Civic Society.

Richard Thackrah and Beryl Falkingham
Addingham, January 2017

Introduction

This book has been a joint effort by Beryl and Richard; Beryl having a lifelong, and deep, interest in, and close family ties to Addingham, and Richard a fascination for the modern and contemporary history of mid-Wharfedale.

Choice has had to feature largely in the variety of material used in the book. Village life, in many ways, was of a similarly varied nature during the war as it had been in peacetime, apart from obvious curtailments of various activities, as shown in people's eyewitness accounts and experiences.

The study of the local history of any locality gives rise to a variety of challenges and surprises.

This book concentrates on the war-related aspects of Addingham life, whereas its companion volume, *'Main Street Memories: Living and shopping in 1940s Addingham'*, details what everyday life was like for those left at home.

The local newspapers, which contained the majority of the material used in the actual wartime sections of this book, provided detailed information about service personnel and government announcements, as well as issues germane to the local community. Censorship existed, but service personnel, individual testament, and letters to the editor, did contain more detail than was published in the national press.

The Wharfe valley in wartime was spoken of as a haven of peace; a place to holiday, convalesce, walk on the moors, take the waters and breathe in unpolluted air. Such views and opinions regularly featured in the papers. This book hints at this situation and provides a view of the social and working lives of many ordinary families in the village, all of whom were patriotic and loyal, to help the nation as a whole to victory in 1945.

As in the First World War, to most men, life in the services was a very new experience. It provided opportunities for service and discipline in new global environments. Addingham men lie buried in Europe and more distant places such as Burma, Canada, Egypt and Tunisia. These brave souls, sixteen of whom sacrificed their lives, gave arduous years of service with profound optimism and a desire to not let down the people at home.

To many people it will be entirely logical to follow up Catherine Snape's scholarly appraisal of the First World War – *"We Who Served... Stories of Addingham and the Great War 1914-18"* – with some examination of the village during the Second World War.

Note that where a street, house, church or another building is mentioned, it is in Addingham unless otherwise stated. Monetary amounts are given in pre-decimal currency: 12 pence (12d) to the shilling (1s) and 20 shillings to the pound (£1). A guinea was one pound and one shilling (£1/1/-).

The following is a timeline of key events in the Second World War, to be read in conjunction with the diary of events in Addingham during those tumultuous and life-changing years:

A World War Two Timeline – 1939-1945

'The Allies' were Britain, France, United States and the Soviet Union
'The Axis' were Germany, Italy and Japan.

1939
1 September: Germany invaded Poland
3 September: Britain and France declared war on Germany

1940
9 April: Denmark and Norway invaded, and occupied, by Germany
10 May: Netherlands, Belgium and France invaded, and occupied, by Germany (Northern France by Germans and Southern France by the Vichy government)
May/June: Dunkirk: evacuation of Allied troops trapped on the beaches
10 June: Italy declared war on France
27 September: Japan concluded Tripartite Pact with Germany and Italy
Mid-July to mid-October: Battle of Britain, followed by the 'Blitz' on London from September 1940 to May 1941
Late 1940: Sheffield, Hull and Middlesborough were bombed – bombing on Hull continued until near the end of the War
1940-1941: German offensive in the Balkans

1941
22 June: Germany invaded the Soviet Union
12 August: The 'Atlantic Charter' was signed by America and Britain: a declaration of common goals for peace
7 December: Surprise attack on Pearl Harbour by Japan wrecked the American Pacific Fleet

1942
11 January: Declaration of the United Nations, signed by the Allied leaders, 'to prosecute war until complete defeat of the Axis powers'
15 February: Fall of Singapore
21 June: Fall of Tobruk
19 August: Failure of the raid on Dieppe
25 October: Battle of El Alamein
November to Feb 1943: Battle of Stalingrad: heavy defeat for Germany and **the tide of war turns against them.**

1943
10 July: Allied invasion of Sicily
3 September: Italy surrenders unconditionally
9 September: Allied landings at Salerno
13 October: Italy declares war on Germany

1944
Various battles in Burma bring some progress for the Allies against the Japanese. Key battles won by British forces were at Imphal and Kohima
22 January: Allied landings at Anzio
18 May: Allies take Monte Cassino after a very hard battle
4 June: Rome captured by the Allies
6 June: 'D-Day': Allied landings in Normandy
13 June: 'V1' flying bomb attacks against Southern England start
20 July: Attempt to kill Hitler narrowly fails and leads to purge of anti-Nazi ringleaders
1 August: 'Warsaw Uprising' – Polish underground resistance crushed by the Germans
15 August: Allied landings in Southern France
17 to 26 September: Failure of airborne assault at Arnhem in The Netherlands
16 December to 25 January 1945: 'Battle of the Bulge': surprise German attack on extended Allied front in Belgium.

1945
4 to 11 February: Yalta conference: Roosevelt, Stalin and Churchill discuss plans for the occupation of Germany after the war
7 March: Allies cross the Rhine
12 April: Americans cross the Elbe
April to June: San Francisco Conference held and the 'United Nations Charter' drawn up
7 May: Germany surrenders
17 July to 2 August: The Potsdam Conference – Truman, Stalin, and Churchill/Attlee outlaw Nazism in Germany, establish Soviet control of Eastern Germany, and call on Japanese to surrender
6 and 9 August: Atomic bombs dropped on Hiroshima and Nagasaki in Japan
2 September: Japan formally surrenders

Post-war treaties were signed in 1947, in Paris, by the Allies and Italy, Romania, Hungary, Bulgaria and Finland
A Peace Treaty with Japan was signed in 1951.

Chapter 1
The Wartime Village

Domestic life and shopping during this period are described in detail in our companion volume *'Main Street Memories'*. Here we concentrate on the war, and civil defence, related activities undertaken to protect the village from the actual and possible dangers of war, and to prepare for post-war life.

The contribution made by villages and small towns the length and breadth of Britain was just as important as the policy waged by the War Cabinet. Whitehall had cause to be grateful to the civilian population of Britain throughout the period from the late summer of 1939 to the late summer of 1945. Addingham was no exception and as attention was turned to preparing for war an appeal for Air Raid Precautions (ARP) personnel was launched and appointments were made of leading officials. Some evacuees arrived from Leeds to the Ilkley district, a blackout was introduced and communal feeding centres were set up. Despite these rapid preparations, the actual declaration of war had been received with quiet soberness in Wharfedale. There was a sense of readiness, as shown by the quick setting up of numerous feeding organisations and, in 1940, the Home Guard (formerly called the Local Defence Volunteers) was created. Addingham was not short of volunteers for this, as the **photo overleaf**, of a group in front of Jack Dixon's poultry-shed, shows.

The Home Guard was trained to use many weapons and increasing exercises in civil defence measures were undertaken. They, and soldiers who were billeted in and around the village, practised manoeuvres in the fields and around the farms, though not always without disturbing the local residents; Phyllis Robinson (who was very young at the time, and lived on Addingham Moorside) remembers a rather unsettling experience: *'One day they really frightened me by entering the house by the back door, running through the room, and out through the front door, to surprise the so called 'enemy', with their guns poised'.* Phyllis said that her Mother grabbed hold of her, and the pram with her twin sisters in, and was, at first, very shocked. *'However, very soon their Commanding Officer severely reprimanded them and apologised to us, as they were not allowed to enter living accommodation while practising'.* (Makes you think of a well-known TV programme!)

Other groups

Demands were made, by the Women's Voluntary Service (WVS), for house accommodation in the district for evacuees from bombed London areas. Rationing began to be introduced and generally operated smoothly. Church bells were silenced, only to be rung on very special occasions during hostilities.

As the war progressed there was a steady increase in numbers joining the three main services and The Special Constabulary, ARP, First Aid Post and Ambulance, the WVS, Evacuee Care, Report Centres, Messenger Corps, the Air Training Corps (ATC) and the Army Cadet Corps were all flourishing. People were also always needed for duty in the Civil Defence Services.

The ARP

It was remarkable how many people, in addition to their industrial work, were working part time in Air Raid Precautions. There were a number of conditions of service for ARP volunteers: they had to be naturally born British subjects, complete prescribed training, could be part or full time, and enrolment was terminable on not less than one week's notice. They acted under the direction of the local authority, were paid emergency rates of pay and any compensation would be paid on conditions laid out at the time.

Life goes on

Climatically, Addingham, and the rest of the UK, had two bad winters during the War, in 1939-40 and 1944-45 and also after the war in 1947. Shortages of food and coal were more pronounced during this period. Generally, in Yorkshire and including Addingham, people were extremely busy; the hours of work long and arduous and the shift hours in the factories and workshops varied by night as well as by day. Throughout the war, much activity in the village was related to the needs of the national war effort, as well as more local edicts.

Petrol restrictions were accepted philosophically but there was criticism of coal rationing, which was generally regarded as unnecessary. Food rationing was introduced in January 1940 and criticism was not more than was likely to be expected in the circumstances. (See *Main Street Memories'* for more about rationing). The vital need for paper salvage was being promoted throughout the district.

Police reported an increase in petty crime since the outbreak of war and this was attributed to the blackout.

The necessity of meeting the demands of modern warfare brought impetus to industry and agriculture, increasingly subject to government supervision, as the country's resources and manpower were geared to winning the war. Soon, the problems of post-war Yorkshire were, to a large extent, the endemic problems of the 20th Century and Addingham, and Wharfedale, were not immune to such changes. Wharfedale was fortunate to suffer no major destruction or casualties: rationing and delays in local planning were the main burdens it had to bear. The need for post-wartime reconstruction, however, meant that Wharfedale people looked forward to the future with a certain amount of apprehension.

By 1940, villagers were raising money for the war effort, welcoming home men who had fought at Dunkirk, and providing shelter, and safety from the blitz, for London evacuees. A year later, villagers were requested to plough up land, including playing fields, for the war effort, but the papers also reported a row over whether Addingham children should attend schools in Silsden or Ilkley/Ben Rhydding. At Christmas 1941 over 160 parcels were sent to Addingham men serving in the forces. Locals were busy throughout the war writing to prisoners-of-war in Germany;

Throughout the war years, Dales villages, such as Addingham, contributed significant sums of money to fund raising activities for comforts for the soldiers, Red Cross parcels, or for war weapons. However, the local council, in spite of the grave situation, managed to give consideration to non-war matters and, from 1943 onwards, were looking ahead to victory and beyond: home and business planning, schooling and social welfare issues started to be given greater consideration at a local level. Poppy Day appeals, for example, began to receive increasing amounts of money, as had numerous wartime financial appeals for military equipment for all three services.

Bombs dropped near Addingham village

Addingham was lucky in having just a few bombs dropped nearby during the war, with minimal damage. Many German bombers, in the early years of the war, were heard overhead at night and the air-raid-warning siren on the Old School would alert the inhabitants of potential danger. It seemed that the bombers used to fly over Wharfedale at night en-route to places such as Belfast, Barrow-in-Furness, Manchester and Liverpool. In 1940, a lone bomber dropped a stick of bombs (i.e. dropped at intervals across target) along the river, starting at Beamsley. The first bomb blew down the gable roof end of a house in Beamsley and the second and third bombs fell in a straight line between Beamsley and Low Mill. The last dropped on the field between Low Mill and Nesfield and made a huge crater. Phyllis Robinson said that her husband Derek, who lived in one of the cottages next to Low Mill, remembered being woken by the explosion. It was fortunate that the

The Wartime Village

bomb did not land on Low Mill and there were no casualties. The Germans obviously, and fortunately, did not realise that a Royal Ordnance factory was in the Skipton area, or that Lancaster bombers were assembled at Yeadon (now Leeds/Bradford Airport)! There was speculation as to whether the bombs were being jettisoned by the bombers on their way home or whether it was meant as a direct hit on Low Mill? What was rather ironic was the fact that an Anglo-German Company, Lister Peltzer, had utilised the mill before the war for velvet production. By July 1939, some of the Germans who were employed at the mill had decided to return home, as war clouds were fast approaching, and some others were taken and interned on the Isle of Man during the war. There had been concern, prior to the outbreak of war, over the number of Germans residing in Wharfedale, many of whom worked for Lister Peltzer at Low Mill.

During the war, by 1941, the velvet looms, which were still operating and employing many local people, were removed to Bradford. Low Mill and its workforce were then used, for the duration of the war, by S.U Carburettors. This was a subsidiary of Morris Motors Ltd, manufacturing aeroplane engine carburettors for the Rolls Royce 'Merlin' engines used in Spitfires and other war planes. After the SU plant at Coventry had been bombed some of the manufacture was transferred to Low Mill and around a thousand men and women were then employed there, from all over the area.

The nearby houses at Sandbeds were taken over by some of the managers in charge of the plant. The mill was quite well guarded, with tall posts alongside the Ilkley Golf Course to protect the plant from low flying planes and the entrance was guarded with machine guns.

This is a photo of the workers at Addingham Low Mill, taken 29 June 1945, showing the last of the range of carburettors which were made there. The photo was kindly forwarded by Mary Readshaw, who is seated on the front row – the first to the left of centre.

Military Training

The moors between the rivers Aire and Wharfe were an ideal training ground for tank units, many of which saw action in North West Europe from 1944 to 1945. Such open ground and rugged terrain taxed the crews! Addingham was one of many places which played host to troops, especially the 15th Scottish Division (227th Infantry Brigade Workshop). A Light Aid Detachment workshop covered the area between Silsden and Ilkley and, instead of repairing tanks, their function was to provide a service for the Infantry Brigade. The 13th (Honourable Artillery Company) Regiment, Royal Artillery, moved to West Yorkshire as part of the 11th Armoured Division for the invasion of Europe, and the Battery was spread over the western edge of Ilkley Moor.

Keeping up morale

The state of morale among villagers continued to be good. There was no spirit of defeatism; instead a clear readiness to face, with fortitude, whatever disasters might be in store. The presence of increasing numbers of troops in the Wharfedale area as the war progressed, particularly from 1943 onwards, had a marked, and tonic, effect on the whole population. Earlier, these self-same people had been grateful to witness the various preparations to resist invasion by airborne troops.

Morale and motivation, as with any village, town or city in wartime, was everything. Propaganda reigned supreme, with the almost daily issuing and promulgation of posters, leaflets, and infinitely proscriptive rules and regulations, seeking to marshal and control thoughts towards the enemy. Blackout regulations were enforced with excessive zeal but this led to burglars benefitting and moving about with much less chance of detection. Addingham was obviously no exception and black marketeers operated; the most universally perpetrated crime of the war. Nearly every person in the country technically fell foul of the onerous regulations at some time during the conflict. Mail was censored and even weather forecasting was curtailed to deny vital information to the enemy. Wireless programmes were reorganised; property requisitioned for military purposes, and travel restricted.

Those at home whilst the men were away fighting took on new roles; women taking on heavy manual work in factories, fields, and on the railways, while older men became air raid wardens and members of the Home Guard, and children helped with the harvest, collected fruit, and acted as messengers and fire watchers. Listening to the radio and reading occupied the relatively brief periods of leisure time, as did visits to the cinema in neighbouring towns. Lack of newsprint did not please avid readers of local and national newspapers. Magazines were also very popular, even though also curtailed in size

The Wartime Village

By late 1939, five Austrian Jewish refugees were given work on farms in the Addingham district. Villagers were sympathetic to the arrival of refugees and evacuees in the district who needed help in the nature of housing, gifts, and money. Full lists of billeting officers and assistants were provided, as well as communal feeding plans in the Ilkley District. In early 1940 the Ministry of Food took over the abattoir to serve a wide area in mid-Wharfedale. One of the early recommendations from the Ministry was to eat more vegetables, 'for your health'.

Health of people, and animals

The Convalescent Home in Ilkley (now Abbeyfield Residential Home) became an emergency hospital for the duration of the war. The new buildings scheme for the Coronation Hospital was put on hold, but not abandoned. There was a growing response to serve in many voluntary organisations. Local savings groups in the area were asked to adopt special financial saving objectives.

By the middle of the war, there were varied issues which required local attention due to the wartime restrictions. Traders were requested to pool deliveries, to use fewer vehicles. Scabies became a notifiable disease and nurses were encouraged to visit schools. Mobile cleansing units were to be provided in the District. Animals were not forgotten: instruction was provided in how to deal with potentially panic-stricken animals during air raids. Farmers were asked to provide more care for sheep on High Moor.

especially in severe weather, and to try and lessen sheep trespass.

1943 witnessed record amounts of money being donated to the 'Wings for Victory' fund to pay for new aircraft. Housewives were also asked to give aluminium pots and pans, for melting down to make aircraft, and wrought-iron railings were cut down for the same reason. Ratepayers demanded better lighting and an end to the poor quality of local roads and, to the surprise of many, it was announced there was going to be a reduction in the number of houses to be erected in Addingham after the war.

Victory in sight

1944 opened with the announcement that the Common Wealth Party had won the Skipton by-election (Addingham, at that time, was in the Skipton constituency and governed by the Skipton Rural Council). A lot more houses were put up for sale and reports about school attendance varied from 'good' to 'bad' during the second half of that year

In 1945 the war ended in Europe and Asia, in May and September respectively. By the autumn of that year, places such as Addingham began to return to the normal way of life that had existed before 1939.

The final year of the war witnessed welcome home events for returning prisoners of war (PoWs), and the advent of peace resulted in VE (Victory in Europe) and VJ (Victory over Japan) Day holidays. The popular tunes of the war were *'Keep the Home Fires Burning'* and *'Bluebirds over the White Cliffs of Dover'*, which was one of Vera Lynn's favourite songs. Church bells now started to be rung on a regular basis, as the war was over. Christmas, and children's birthdays, which were always well celebrated during the dark war years, were now to assume greater significance in the new world of peace.

At the end of the war, Polish troops were sent to Ilkley to clear parts of the Moor of ordnance and any explosive materials: acres of Rombald's Moor had been under Army control for military training.

Despite a certain amount of apprehension about the future, which was understandable, Wharfedale people could be proud of what they had achieved in their own small way for the overall war effort. Their labours and sacrifices would never be forgotten and are, like those for every village, town, and city in the UK, remembered each November.

A general discussion took place in 1946 about the proposed erection of a war memorial in the village. Bringing the horrors of war even closer to many people in Addingham was the involvement of family members and friends in combat with the enemy in different theatres of war, and the loss of 16 men whilst serving their country. For those who returned home safely there was relief and joy, but for 16 families and their relations, there was much sadness. This book commemorates those 16 men particularly.

Those who returned home exchanged their uniform for a full suit of clothes and often these were made by the Leeds company Montague Burton

The first Ilkley Agricultural Show started as a result of a successful show linked with 'Holidays at Home' week and this proved very popular with farmers in the area.

A profound legacy

No event in history had such a profound and long term effect as the Second World War: its consequences are still shaping the modern world and, moreover, the war years were frightening for ordinary civilians. People responded to the challenge with incredible fortitude, camaraderie, determination and good humour, and this applied to the people of Addingham and in Wharfedale, as to other towns, villages, and districts around the UK. Factory workers, allotment holders, farmers, and the emergency services, just carried on as if nothing unusual had happened.

Chapter 2
LOCAL NEWSPAPERS AND NEWS IN WARTIME

When one studies local history and has the privilege of looking at paper copies of one's own local newspaper, one can easily get carried away with a whole series of 'ed' words: one has explored, discovered, found, connected, engaged, unearthed, learned, imagined, created, unlocked, opened, revealed and celebrated – in this case the history of an iconic town, solely from the pages of the *Ilkley Gazette,* since 1868(and, in Addingham's case, the *Craven Herald* and *West Yorkshire Pioneer* also). The *'Gazette'* was first published in May 1861, but the first eight years of the paper are unfortunately lost or unavailable.

Since the mid-19th Century, wood pulp came into Great Britain from a number of countries, including Norway until the Nazis invaded that country on 9 April 1940 and the importation of newsprint and wood pulp then stopped. Paper was rationed from September 1939 and newspapers limited in the amount that they could use. The 'Control of Paper Order' came into effect in the spring of 1940 and circulation numbers were restricted to the then-prevailing level for the duration of the war. By 1945, newspapers were limited to 25% of their pre-war consumption so a drastic reduction in the number of pages per issue was inevitable, with news reports, therefore, limited in length.

In spite of economies borne out of necessity, local newspaper editors continued to present, fairly and accurately, items of local news. It was common for these to appear in summarised form with items of minor importance eliminated and, if other changes had to be made as a result of the Order, the paper would ask for the indulgence of its readers.

In the papers, one can read about war's impact on the Home Front, how people amused themselves in the face of adversity, and the way in which public morale was kept high through a mixture of propaganda and judicious reporting. The papers told of the hopes and fears of the British people at large, air raids, blackouts, the destruction of property, the evacuation of children, the loss or absence of loved ones, rationing and conscription. These were that generation's lot, but life just carried on.

People had an appetite for local as well as national news and both types of newspaper carried out the wishes of government in keeping up morale. The UK was, economically and emotionally, drained by the war at national, regional, and local level. Local papers also showed how news of world events could be mirrored and expressed to the people.

People lived with the constant fear of attack, and families often became divided as a result of the fighting. Thousands worked very long hours, often volunteering their little free time to help the war effort as well as keeping normal jobs, but there was a worry that people on the Home Front might grow disillusioned with the war and that this could lead to defeat. Local officials used censorship and propaganda to maintain the morale of the citizens during the war. It was felt that keeping secret certain details which might cause people to lose hope would be best for the morale of the country.

Here follow extracts from the local papers that specifically refer to Addingham, culled from the original archived copies.

A wartime diary of local news reports, week by week

The following reports appeared in the local press during the period 1939 – 1946. The initials at the end indicate which paper they came from: (CH)=Craven Herald, (IG)=Ilkley Gazette, (WYP)=West Yorkshire Pioneer

1939

6 January	The Conservative Club and Catholic Church hold one of their regular whist drives (IG)
13 January	Parish Council: regarding the shocking state of roads in village – Rose Terrace and Victoria Terrace (IG)
	Change in County Electoral Divisions – Addingham to be included in the Staincliffe Division (IG)
	Mrs E Bartholomew dies; she was an Addingham Parish Church worker (IG)
	National Farmers Union (NFU), Addingham & Ilkley branch, hold one of their regular whist drives (IG)
3 February	Air Raid Precautions: organisations in the area are worried by so many instructions, circulars and regulations emanating from Whitehall that there is hardly time to read them (CH)
10 February	Jack Coppen (36), well known Addingham motor engineer, is killed in a car crash at Riddlesden when his car turned over and crushed him (IG/CH)
	Mr B Blake, head of Addingham National School for 7 years up to 1932, dies (IG)
	Local distribution of the National Service Guide completed (IG)
	Test of air raid sirens throughout Skipton and Settle police districts to take place on 15 February and public are asked to adhere to instructions (CH)
	Appeal for food and clothing for victims of the Spanish Civil War – message from Skipton and Area League of Nations Union (CH)
17 February	Empire Day Career Campaign Appeal allowed in Addingham (IG)
	'Mr and Mrs Cheer' – presentation by Addingham Athletic

	Club for creating team spirit in the club (IG) Addingham Cricket Club in sound financial position (IG), Tribute to Mr E Mason, from Addingham Athletic Club, as he leaves to join the RAF (IG)
17 February	Mr W Bradley of Addingham is exhibiting at the Exhibition of Inventions in London, a precisely controlled friction clutch and the design of an automatic cloth-folding machine designed to fold cloth or artificial silk in any desired length (CH) (Note: see *Bill Bradley, Addingham's Most Inventive Engineer* by Don Barrett & Ian Crawshaw) 1938 was a year of bad trade for agriculture, with problems for tenant farmers (CH)
24 February	Addingham lady climbs the Franz Josef glacier in New Zealand (CH)
10 March	Air Raid Precautions: Apart from Silsden, other units are now at full strength (CH) Food for cattle in wartime: Craven farmers emphasise home production (CH)
17 March	Addingham Parish Church ladies' working party hold one of their regular meetings (IG) Parish Council: critics of proposal for a new school to be built in Ilkley (CH) A scheme to spend £50,000 (subject to a satisfactory grant from central funds) on construction of air raid shelters near schools, for children and general public, approved by West Riding County Council (WRCC) (CH)
31 March	Complaints by Moorside residents of need for repairs to the road from Scargill to Cragg House, and footpath at Smallbanks (Gildersber) (IG) Walter Roe dies. He was an ex-Addingham resident and well-known pig dealer (IG)
6 April	Agreed, at Parish Council meeting, to write to the Rural Council concerning the road from Scargill to Cragg House (IG)
7 April	Dr John P Senior of Ilkley appointed Examining Surgeon, under Factories Act 1937, in succession to Dr Bates (resigned), in the village district (CH)
14 April	Alice Mason, of Reynard Ing on the Moorside, marries Robert Vert of Glasgow at Addingham Parish Church (IG)
21 April	Installation of new water turbine at Low Mill, which replaces

the old water wheel, and the finding of an old coin, dated 1806, under the headrace arch leading to the old water wheel. These were mentioned in current issue of 'Lister's Magazine' (IG)

Joseph Roe dies in Addingham, aged 66. He used to ride the horse which pulled a wagonette, for visitors' use, at Bolton Abbey, (IG)

Appeal to Skipton district farmers to give an opportunity to German, non-Jewish, refugees to acquire a practical knowledge of farm work (CH)

197 children in Addingham taking subsidiary nourishment- applies to all Addingham and Beamsley schools (CH)

For the first time on Civic Sunday, in the Skipton district, Air Raid Precautions (ARP) personnel (wardens and other workers) took part in the Civic Procession (CH)

28 April — Complaints at Addingham Parish Council meeting about the slackness of the authorities in their arrangements for Air Raid Precautions work in Addingham (IG)

12 May — Addingham water supply described as 'dreadful' at Parish Council meeting, plus complaints of overflowing dustbins (CH)

Parish Council: the application for a resident Registrar in Addingham had Skipton Rural Council's full support (CH)

26 May — 4,500 rural area evacuees for Skipton district, and plans for their reception in emergency (CH)

9 June — Mothers' Union annual outing was to Scarborough this year (IG)

Craven area ARP wardens are to be provided with their own monthly newspaper (CH)

Addingham District Education Order received that, if and when necessary to evacuate school children, the schools would be closed for 7 days as a national emergency measure. If this measure were taken during a holiday, then teachers would return to school at once. 215 persons from the Bradford district would be evacuated to Addingham (CH)

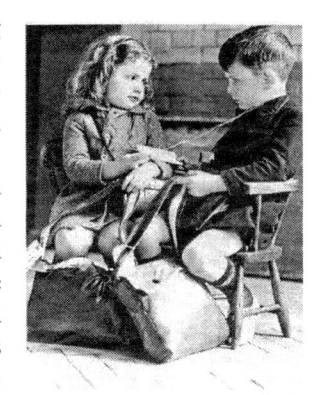

Evacuees

23

16 June	Two air raid warden posts for village, says Parish Council – based in Council Room and in the harness room at Hallcroft Hall (CH)
23 June	Mr J T Moran of Burley and Miss Anna C (Nan) Mason, of Reynard Ing, married in Ilkley, at Church of Sacred Heart (IG)
14 July	Moorside Road: Rural Council wrote to the Parish Council to say it was an 'occupation road' and therefore repairable by the owner (IG)
21 July	Letter from "Old Echo" to Ilkley Gazette: 'How many Germans are presently resident in Addingham and Ilkley area? Are those Germans, who reside in the district and who are not naturalised, doing work which could be of National importance?' (IG)
28 July	Supplies of special respirators for small children and anti-gas protective helmets for babies will be available in WRCC area from August, says West Riding Chief Constable (CH)

News in Wartime

4 August	National camps for summer school purposes, or for evacuation purposes in War, are to be provided in many places in North England – Wharfedale's will be at Linton (CH) Allan Mason, 18-year-old left arm medium pace bowler, was selected to play for Yorkshire 2nd XI in various matches in August (CH)
11 August	Less land being used for agriculture in England & Wales than in 1930.
18 August	Well-known local flautist Roy Richardson is to give a second radio broadcast, from the Leeds studio of the BBC, on 25 August. He is a member of the Skipton Permanent Orchestra (IG) Demands for a post box to serve Addingham residents, but at Smallbanks there could be a letter box although this has been sought by just 4 people!(CH)
1 September	Addingham Athletic Club: sports and games, arranged by National Fitness Committee, held in Ilkley on 26 August 1939, were a great success (IG). Skipton Rural Council to take 3,354 evacuee children (CH) Senior ARP Wardens for Addingham: Mr Edward Holmes, Hallcroft, Mr J B Ives, Holme House, Mr William Whitaker, 8 Moor Lane, and Mr Charles Newton, 13 Moor Lane (CH)
8 September	500 evacuees to West Craven; no more at present (CH) Appeals for nurses by Women's Voluntary Service (WVS); volunteers sought for Craven District (CH)
15 September	Addingham's lack of equipment for fighting fires in the event of an air raid were subject of lively discussion at Parish Council meeting on 11 September. 'Plenty of volunteers but no tackle' and 'villages would be burned to the ground' (IG) Parish Council: fire hydrants in village should be painted white and a white mark painted on walls or hedges to denote where they were (CH)
6 October	Addingham Parish Church: a day of prayers (decided by the Archbishop). Emphasis made on the need for sincere prayer (IG)

An ARP Warden with stirrup pump

20 October	Evacuees drift back home (CH)
3 November	As a result of a fortnightly dance, held at the Crown Club Room on 27 October, a sum of 25s handed over to Women's Knitting Circle for efforts to supply extras for Addingham boys serving with the Forces (IG)
17 November	23 Addingham men now in forces. Later, on 1 December, 14 replied with thanks for letters of appreciation (CH)
24 November	Addingham Athletic Club: Aircraftsman Eric Mason, who joined RAF in March, is an AAC member. Mason passed his physical training instructors exam with honours at the school of physical training (IG) Construction of a new trunk road around Addingham, Burley, Ilkley and Otley has been postponed due to the war (IG) Ilkley and Addingham raised £364/11/6d, which was £51 in excess of the previous total, for Remembrance Sunday (IG)
1 December	William Henry Smith, ambulance man for 60 years, dies in Addingham (CH)
15 December	Addingham wall repaired with help from boys who damaged it! (CH)
22 December	Picture of Women's Knitting/Sewing Party carrying out valued work in making comforts for Addingham men serving in Forces (IG) *(see p.108)* Gifts of wool, knitted goods, cash, picture-papers and magazines, left at Conservative Club in Addingham (IG) H Blakeney Flynn and twin brothers George and Jack Stapleton have joined up (IG)

1940

5 January	Addingham: New School for Juniors. Site negotiations suspended during the War's duration (CH) Women's' Knitting Circle: three shillings, in postal orders, sent to Addingham men in forces (CH)
12 January	Addingham Parish Council meeting: ARP complaint regarding rent for Post that no one will pay; they deplored treatment received from local headquarters in Skipton. Payment was eventually authorised for rent for Conservative Club Room as an ARP Post (CH) Following the receipt of a letter from West Riding War

News in Wartime

	Agricultural Committee asking Parish Council to encourage food production on allotments, it was mentioned that several allotment gardens in the village were untenanted (CH)
19 January	Women's Knitting Circle entertained to supper and whist drive in the music room of Farfield Hall by Mr George Douglas. Knitting Circle Whist Drive raised cash, again, for forces' comforts (CH)
26 January	Brumfit Atkinson (right), First World War veteran, of Victoria Terrace, dies, aged 61, on 24 January.(CH/IG) (*See 'We who Served…' by Catherine Snape – Ed*)
2 February	Below zero temperatures in Ilkley area. Addingham people handicapped as all travelling facilities dislocated and difficult to get to and from work. Particularly bad on the Skipton and Bolton Abbey side of village (IG) Successful dance and whist drive held by First Aid Post (IG)
9 February	£20 raised for Addingham First Aid Post through its self-organised whist drive and dance (CH)
16 February	Mr T Lancaster joined RAF, from Athletic Club (IG)
1 March	Cricket Club members who play in 1940 almost same number as in 1939, even though some members were in Forces (IG)
8 March	Carnival Dance raised £3 for men serving in Forces, from Addingham (IG)
15 March	Edward Holmes resigns from Addingham Parish Council after objecting to the women who run the First Aid Post in Conservative Club having to pay rent of 2s per week out of own efforts when there is a charge on rates for ARP work (IG) Terms for modified street lighting in Addingham, at cost of 15/6d per lamp, and price of gas was £2/15/4d per lamp for 20 lamps for 260 days (16 August 1940–22 April 1941) (CH)
29 March	Fine display of Northern Lights seen in Wharfedale on 24 March 1940 (IG)
12 April	Possibility of a library for Addingham, with a motion passed by members at the Parish Council meeting to 'pay a penny and two-fifths rate for library purposes' (IG) Addingham knits for Forces: over 500 articles already supplied (IG)

19 April	Parish Council Officers: 'In regard to distribution of gas masks for babies, a letter from District Council intimated that the Rural Authority were responsible for primary arrangements and that it was Air Raid Wardens' duty to distribute them' (CH)
26 April	Knitting Group: Mr J. Dickson a prize winner (IG) Budget, 23 April 1940: Reform of purchase tax – details later in the year. Beer 1d a pint more, whisky 1s/9d a bottle, tobacco 3d an ounce, matches ½d on a box of 50, postage: 2½d letters, 2d postcards, 3d foreign, Telephone charge: 15% up (one shilling call now 1s/2d). Telegraph rate: fixed, an additional charge of 3d on each ordinary, priority, or greeting telegram. Income tax increased from 7s to 7/6d in the pound. Entertainments: Duty to be increased by ½d on theatre prices up to 1/10d. Purchase tax: Present bill was withdrawn and luxury tax of 24% on articles, including clothing, boots, and shoes (CH) First Aid Post raised net sum of £25/5/11d, which helped to pay rent of room and to purchase equipment (CH)
10 May	Lumb Beck Farm (below): large attendance for its sale by Mr F M Lister. When bidding reached £775, property was withdrawn (IG)

17 May	Whitsun holidays in Addingham same as usual: closure of mills on Monday and Tuesday (IG) Frank Hartley dies aged 51. He served in Kitchener's Army (IG)

News in Wartime

24 May	Parish Council asks for two police constables to be regularly stationed in the village (IG) Parish Council heard that West Riding Chief Constable refused to increase the number of constables in Addingham (CH) Hopefully, ARP Wardens could have room rent free as no claim for rental would be approved by WRCC unless the Parish Council could prove a loss of revenue (CH)
14 June	How village can help the war: old metal, 'Pig Clubs', a lending library and a National War Savings Campaign concerning formation of a War Savings Group in village (IG) Parish Council: secretary and treasurer of local savings group to be put in place (CH) Rural Council requested Parish Council to consider appointing an organiser regarding collecting old metal in the village (CH)
21 June	Private G Stapleton describes his experiences in France and Belgium and his retreat from Dunkirk: *'All the time machine-gunned, shelled and bombed. Only one lift-on transport lorry, and that was in Belgium. Walked about thirty miles a day on one meal and four hours sleep. Sometimes dig trenches at night and then walk next day. Regularly had to avoid Germans bombing and shelling the beach at Dunkirk; as soon as one lot dived another appeared. Had to wade up to waists to get into the water. Very relieved to see Dover's White Cliffs'* (CH)
28 June	George and Jack Stapleton home from Dunkirk. They are both Privates, who lived at 'Westcliffe', Moor Lane. They were in Bethune in Belgium and lost touch until home. George was in Dunkirk several days and thirty planes bombed and machine-gunned them (IG) Ben Rishworth and Henry Tennant evacuated from Dunkirk. Ronald Moore and Peter Pringle are in Norway (IG)
5 July	Private Charlie Allen, who lives at 12 Church Street, is reported missing. Called up September 1939 and went with Northumberland Fusiliers to France in May 1940. Aged 21, he worked at Listers' Low Mill, in the village. Active in St. John Ambulance, he played football for Addingham and the British Legion Club, Ilkley; is a bell ringer in Parish Church and a member of Addingham Athletic Club (IG) Athletic Club gets involved in collecting scrap (CH)
12 July	Signaller Walter Millman marries. He was later a Japanese

Addingham in World War Two

	PoW (CH)
	Addingham library mix-up over appointment of a librarian: a post is not to be advertised (CH)
	Approval was given to investing in War Bonds of cash which was the balance in the local lighting account (CH)
19 July	Knitting Circle members doing a good job in collecting aluminium for the war effort (CH)
26 July	At a Military Whist Drive, Mr J Dickson represented 'India' and won a prize for coming second to 'Switzerland' (IG)
	Parish Council meeting: Agriculture War Emergency Committee stresses need for cultivation of all allotments and unused building land and asks for Council co-operation on this matter (CH)
16 August	Parish Council: importance of drains, and complaints about allotment cultivation (IG)
6 September	A stick of bombs from a lone German plane fell near Low Mill, Addingham, on 4 September. (IG)
	Mrs Laumen (her parents, Mr and Mrs Samuel Waters, resided in Ash Grove, Ilkley) is home after 14 weeks internment in the Isle of Man. In 1937 she married a German, Mr J K. Laumen, from Krefeld in Germany (known as the 'Velvet or Silk City'), who was employed by the Lister Peltzer Company, an early manufacturer of velvet in both Addingham and Krefeld. Mr and Mrs Laumen had been interned on security grounds. Later, Mr Laumen was on the liner Arandora Star, taking German and Italian prisoners across the Atlantic, which was sunk by a U-boat, but he survived and was brought back to Britain. Mrs Laumen has two brothers: her eldest was in the RAF in Egypt and her youngest in the Royal Artillery in Scotland (IG)
13 September	Collection being organised, with Girl Guide help, in aid of St Dunstan's Hostel (IG)
	Addingham farmer fined 20 shillings for failing to immobilise his car (CH)
8 October	Overtime pay in ARP varied even between areas in Yorkshire and solution is 'by no means free from difficulty' (CH)
25 October	Pay for weavers: conditions can be different in weaving areas from those in spinning areas.
	'Roof spotting' system, recommended by Government, is approved and endorsed (CH)
	Where air raid shelters are provided on the premises, the time

	lost will be calculated from the 'cease work' signal until not more than 15 minutes after signal to resume work (CH)
15 November	Discussion by Parish Council over what the library will cost (IG)
	Service of homage at Parish Church (CH)
	Poppy Day: record sum reached £27/5/4d (CH)
22 November	Mr G Dickson made gift to Knitting Circle (CH/IG)
13 December	Over 40 evacuees in the village, including several young children: Parish Council said they could meet in the library on Monday, Tuesday, and Thursday, 1.30-4.30pm. They needed a place to meet, particularly on wet days (IG)
20 December	Christmas parcels sent to ninety-nine men and one woman from Addingham, who are serving in HM Forces in Europe, and four postal orders to men serving in the Middle East and the Far East. House-to-house collection: £32/9/½d raised by Knitting Circles. Tea provided to circle members in Conservative Club, by Mr and Mrs Hillman (IG)

1941

3 January	Addingham Athletic Club are helping the Women's Knitting Circle and are organising a football team to play a Royal Horse Artillery team, to raise fund for the ladies (IG)
10 January	Mr Ellis Kettlewell dies, aged 62. He served in the Royal Engineers in the First World War (IG)
17 January	Parish Council heard calls of an urgent need for a Registrar of Births and Deaths in Addingham, as well as progress made in Auxiliary Fire Services, and establishment of a welfare centre for troops (IG)
	A social evening held by members of First Aid Post: Miss J Hillman acted as accompanist (IG)
	The Chaplain to the Forces, Rev Ronald Royal MC CF, preached at the Parish Church on 12 January on 'the sanctity of the Christian family, in spite of present difficult times when so many families are parted for reasons of service and safety' (IG)
31 January	Start of charges for repairs to Addingham gas masks, except for rubber bands and valves (IG)
	Public meeting in the village to explain a scheme for

Addingham in World War Two

	protection against incendiary bombs. All responsible male citizens, with the exception of those serving in civil defence, are expected to attend (IG) Mid-January snow blizzard: serious inconvenience caused in Craven (CH)
7 February	A meeting held to arrange a scheme for Fire Guards, and systematic patrols in Addingham in case of air raid warnings (IG) ARP post at The Old School considerably understaffed, being seven men short of the full complement (IG) Fire party arrangement under review: village divided into 12 sections and volunteers to take up duty were needed (CH)
14 February	At a meeting on 10 February, Parish Council arranged for electric siren to be fitted on Old School Building (IG) Further meeting, in Old School *(below)*, which had, for its objective, enrolment of volunteers for firefighting services in village, had a better attendance, including some women (IG) Need for improvement to blackout and there was the issue of the railway station lights (CH)
21 February	Whist drive at National School benefits First Aid Post funds (CH) Mr George Douglas, of Farfield Hall, has donated money towards one of eight mobile canteens to be operated in West Riding (CH)
28 February	Soldier John Stephenson, of Royal Horse Artillery, then based in Silsden, was knocked down and killed while walking on the

News in Wartime

	road between Addingham and Silsden on 22 February. He had just alighted from a bus (IG) For Addingham firefighters, a practical demonstration (nearby) of how to deal with incendiary bombs and fires (IG) 119 Addingham men now serving with forces. Young men in Craven generally show preference for the RAF (CH)
14 March	Parish Council discussed the formation of a flight of the Air Training Corps in the village, for boys aged 16 to 18, if there are sufficient boys to do ATC work in the village. If not it would have to go to Ilkley. They also discussed the need for a resident Registrar and the provision of an air raid siren. (CH)
28 March	Girl from Addingham and boy from Ilkley badly injured when cycling. They collided with a car in Ben Rhydding, at the point of Wheatley Lane junction with the road to Ben Rhydding Golf Hotel. (IG)
4 April	Addingham Council has a letter from the District Council about purchasing a mobile canteen for Skipton Division. Councillors present gave £7 to give the movement for the canteen a start (IG)
11 April	Call for reinforcement of air raid sirens in Addingham District, by Parish Council. Council also requested a renewed application for a deputy Registrar of births and deaths to be appointed in village, rather than people having to go to Skipton (IG)
18 April	Passion play 'The Upper Room', by Robert Benson, was given in National School on Maundy Thursday and Good Friday (IG) New centre for blood donors in village opened at First Aid Post in the Conservative Club (IG) Quiet Easter holiday; fewer visitors in Craven area (IG)
2 May	No new siren allowed for Addingham as village not badly placed regarding air raid warnings (IG) Due to supporters' endeavours, Cricket Club can continue, at least for 1941 season (CH)
2 May	Dr W C Crabtree re-elected as Chairman of the Parish Council (CH)
9 May	Knitting Circle: Mrs W. Dickson gave a gift (CH)
23 May	The first of the new film-copied letters from the Middle East has reached Mr and Mrs C Hargreaves of 'Midway', Addingham, from their son Kenneth (IG)

(Note: 'film-copied' letters were Airgraph forms upon which letters were written and then photographed and sent home as rolls of microfilm. They were then printed on photographic paper and delivered through the normal Royal Engineers' Postal Section, also known as the Army Postal Services, systems.)

Names of Eric Dickson and others added to the list of Addingham men serving in forces. It now totals 143 (CH)

PoW Adoption: fortnightly meeting takes place; by subscribing £1 a year for each member of the circle, the Red Cross will be able to send a 10s parcel, at intervals, to the adopted prisoner (CH)

30 May	Captain S N Carter, Company Commander of Addingham Home Guard from the inception of the force until April 1941, received leather toilet case in appreciation. He has now received an appointment in the regular army (IG)
6 June	145 Addingham men now serving in forces, with additions of W Fairbrother and Eric Smith (IG)
13 June	Possibility of swings, bowls and tennis in Memorial Close (IG)
27 June	Torpedoed ship survivor Mrs Florence Campbell, daughter of Mr and Mrs Thomas Bradley, Riversleigh, Addingham. Mr Campbell was on Parish Council some 17 years ago. Mrs Campbell had visited various parts of the world with her husband, who was engaged in laying out sugar plantations. They spent 9 days in an open boat after the ship on which they were travelling was torpedoed. Rescued by another ship, only to be torpedoed a second time after 3 days, with a further 13 days in an open boat and, above all, she had seen nothing of her husband since the second boat sank. Mr Campbell and 15 other men went down with the ship. 56 people, including Mrs Campbell, were in a lifeboat with many foreigners, including several Chinese sailors, with just 1½ biscuits and a drop of tinned milk as a daily ration. They continued for 13 days, experiencing terrific storms, and one man, who went mad, jumped overboard and was immediately taken by a shark. They then saw a ship and signalled it with the only flashlamp on the boat and it was another British ship. They had travelled circa 500 miles during 13 days in the second open boat. They were then transferred to a British Hospital ship and got home without further incident. (IG)
4 July	George Dickson, a member of Knitting Circle, added to list of Addingham men in forces – now totals 148 (IG) (See

News in Wartime

Chapter 3)

11 July	Mrs Margaret Wall (34) was found drowned in High Mill Dam (IG)
18 July	Should senior scholars in Addingham, on leaving primary school, go to Silsden Modern School or continue at Senior School in Ben Rhydding? (IG)
1 August	Signalman Sydney Ratcliffe RN missing in Mediterranean while on convoy duty. He was due to marry Miss Joan Wilkinson, of Addingham, at Christmas 1941 (IG)
	Addingham scholars to attend a Silsden School, under major reorganisations of schools. Addingham parents voted 41 to 14 to abide by WRCC scheme for such a transfer. Eventually, when a new school is built in Ilkley, (delayed by the War) those children from Addingham at Silsden School can go to school in Ilkley (IG)
	181 people from Addingham now in Forces (CH)
12 September	Parish Council agreed to the playing field being ploughed, after a request from Skipton branch of War Agricultural Committee. The Government would grant a subsidy of £2 per acre and implements are provided to plough up about three acres (IG)
	Knitting Circle appeals for more Christmas parcels in 1941 (IG)
15 September	Final arrangements by the County to take over a room in the village for a library (CH)
19 September	Gunner Readshaw, of Stockinger Lane, writes letter to say, *'Keep the old flag flying – am sticking the heat and hope to survive'*
	High praise for all members at an Air Training Corps camp in the village, from the visiting secretary of the West Riding Territorial and Air Force Association. He praised all the 16 to 18-year-old members, especially as they had had little training as a unit (CH)
26 September	Mr Charles Roberts, of Addingham, gave 19 Barbizon and Dutch pictures to the Leeds Art Gallery in 1937 and has now given his collection of porcelain, pottery and furniture. It is to be exhibited at Temple Newsam in Leeds until the end of the war (IG)
3 October	Miss Joy Clarkson, 9-year-old Addingham girl, raised £2/13s by herself in aid of Knitting Circle funds (IG)
24 October	159 Christmas parcels to be sent to members of the forces

	from Addingham (CH)
31 October	Addingham public bodies agreed to raise funds for YWCA (namely: all Churches, Home Guard, First Aid and Nursing Association and the Athletic Club) (CH)
7 November	Mr Whitham, in the Ilkley Auxiliary Fire Service and a former member of the Addingham Auxiliary Fire Service and Addingham Cricket Club, rescued people from a blazing vehicle full of fuel (the 'Menston bus disaster'). His father is a grocer in Main Street (CH)
21 November	Addingham man poisons himself with ammonia: found lying dead in a field near Winebeck Farm (IG)
28 November	40 names handed in to be members of a newly established Youth Centre in Addingham. A wide range of cultural, educational, religious and recreational activities will eventually be organised (IG)
5 December	Transfer of Addingham pupils to Silsden School has now happened. Need for school meals provision in all Addingham schools (IG)
19 December	Youth organisation, widely representative, now moving forward (IG)
26 December	Mr T. Hardaker, a nephew of Mr Holmes of Addingham, escaped from Germany in 1941, by way of occupied France, to reach England, with his wife and daughter. He resided in Paris as a representative for a Bradford wool firm in France. He had been taken to Germany after the Nazis occupied Paris in June 1940 (IG)

1942

2 January	When one writes to a PoW in Germany, remember that there are censors whose duty is to read all letters sent home by prisoners themselves, or coming in from relatives and friends. Write clearly and be precise about which Stalag (German for permanent camp) in letter and number. Better to have letters typed, no more than two a week, and keep them brief. Be careful regarding enclosures – normally just personal mounted, or un-mounted, photos and simple bank account statements. Airgraph letters from relatives serving in the Middle East cannot be forwarded to PoWs in Germany. It is strictly forbidden to give the address of one's own unit at home/overseas if writing to a relative in PoW camps and

News in Wartime

serving in Forces in UK. Instead, he should state address of relative or friend in the UK who would be willing to send on any letters received from his friend behind barbed wire in a camp in Germany. Do not communicate with prisoners through people in neutral countries. Rules are necessary and following them can expedite transmission of mail to and from those of your relatives and friends who are PoWs (IG)

Christmas holidays are used by many people to raise funds for Red Cross Fund, and for the Middleton Sanatorium and Emergency Hospital (IG)

9 January   Addingham man, Private Jack Hartley of Moor Lane, is recovering from an eye operation caused by accident while playing football. A Harley Street specialist performed the operation and he is now at convalescent camp (IG)

Young Women's Christian Association appeal for funds led to £60/6/5d being raised (IG)

16 January   Addingham Parish Council ordered the ploughing up of the cricket pitch to be utilised for a crop of grain (IG)

Paper salvage is important and any books are also vital for salvage (IG)

Complaints regarding scavenging, and agreed that ashbins are to be emptied weekly and ash pits once a month (IG)

23 January   Local MP, Sir Granville Gibson (MP for Pudsey and Otley division), concerned about absenteeism on New Year's Day: in 1942 this accounted for 47.08% workforce or 56,944 tons of coal, which was urgently needed (IG)

Scrap iron for the war effort: farmers can give help in this endeavour by providing details of the weight of scrap, where it is situated, and how it can be collected by the authorities (CH)

30 January   Will all parents whose offspring were born prior to 31 March 1937, return their small child's respirator, which is more suitable for children of 5 years of age than the 'Mickey Mouse' respirator (right). 20 parents still have such respirators and will be charged for them, if not returned (IG)

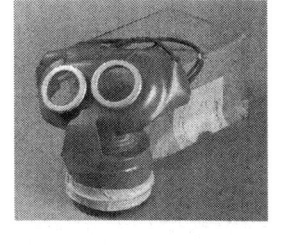

Disastrous barn fire on Main Street caused £400 worth of damage to the building (CH)

6 February	Addingham scholars at Silsden School are receiving good meals, both in quality and variety (IG)
8 February	The Home Guard held a social function at the Swan Hotel when a large gathering of members was served with light suppers and played darts and dominoes during the remainder of the evening. Mr B Hustwick was on piano. Organisers: Sergeant Clarkson and Corporal Stocks (IG)
13 February	Knitting Circle are busy knitting pullovers, socks and helmets for Russia (IG) Parish Council asked for a second telephone box to be installed in the village centre (IG)
20 February	Aid to Russia: Mrs Churchill's Aid to Russia Fund, dance and whist drive at the First Aid Post and from counters in Co-op Store, raised £32/6s/6d in total (IG) Local NFU (Addingham/Ilkley branch) made an appeal for scrap iron and, on many farms, metal oddments, which the nation required (CH)
27 February	John James Cowgill dies. He was one of Addingham's best-known tradesmen (CH)
13 March	Telephone kiosk is to be erected in School Yard (IG)
20 March	Gunner Jack Stones: his wife in Addingham has been told that her husband is missing in Malaya. He had been on board a ship now reported lost, and he had already served on two ships which had been sunk (IG)
	Royal Marine Bandsman Hedley Adams, of Cragg View, is reported missing. A musician since Ilkley Grammar School days, playing the violin, piano and saxophone, a good swimmer, and a member of Ilkley Players. His father is director of James Adams Ltd, dress goods manufacturer, and Cricket Club Member. Hedley has been in Navy 2 years (CH)
27 March	Ernest Turnpenny, aged 28, husband of Mrs Ethel Turnpenny, is missing. In civilian life, he was employed by Bradford Dyers Assn. An old boy of Ilkley Grammar School, he joined up two years ago and went overseas in early October. His only brother is serving on a Minesweeper. (IG) Signaller Walter Millman is also missing, his wife lives at Lodge Hill. He joined up 1940 and was an electrician for Messrs. Innes and a Cricket Club member. He has been overseas for a year (IG) Recently formed Addingham Youth Council elects all its

	officers (IG)
3 April	Geoffrey Wall, 21 months old, was scalded when he climbed into a bath of hot water at his home, and died from extensive scalds, in Bradford Children's Hospital (IG) Home Guard help Red Cross raise £24 at a whist drive and dance (IG)
10 April	Quietest Easter on record: few holidaymakers in Craven. Officials of the recently formed Youth Council are getting to work. They hoped to have a permanent centre in the village where young people can meet (CH) Addingham gassing tragedy: the death of Miss Mary Jane Wilkinson, aged 63, a cotton weaver who had lost the ability to smell. She was found suffering from coal gas poisoning at her home in Main Street (CH)
17 April	Addingham man, aged 37, shot dead in his bedroom in Johannesburg, South Africa. Rev. John (Vincent) Wall, Warden, St Peter's Hostel, Rottenville, was the son of Mr Foster Wall of Main Street. He served in Zululand, then home to Community of Resurrection at Mirfield, and finally to the native training school of St Peter's near Johannesburg (IG) Concern at Parish Council over footpaths on land which had been ploughed up and, in some cases, paths were also ploughed up. Stated in Council that people can still walk on these paths (IG) Vandalism at Memorial Close: rollers removed, and wire netting out, next to the bowling green (IG)
24 April	District Nursing Association AGM: stated that during the year the nurses had paid 3,147 visits, including 1,431 general visits, 514 maternity, 507 health, 323 antenatal, 60 school and 312 casual visits. 232 patients were attended to (IG)
8 May	Mrs S Warr, of Ilkley, retires after 21 years as assistant mistress at the Addingham National School (IG)
15 May	Tennis court 'so little used that it did not pay for the whitewash to mark it out' (IG) Parents in Addingham asked when the provision of a mid-day meal would begin. They were told that the mobile canteen is fully employed and Addingham would have to make its own arrangements. Question of providing meals at High Council School under consideration (CH)
25 May	Dividend of 2s in £1 approved at the half-yearly meeting of Addingham Cooperative Society (CH)

12 June	Damage to property in Memorial Close, especially to trees and a tool house (CH)
19 June	Fred Shackleton, aged 28, youngest son of Mr and Mrs Shackleton of Main Street, is in hospital in Northumberland. Whilst serving on a destroyer, he suffered injuries to his eyes and face as a result of an accident. His wife received urgent telegram to go there immediately. In a letter to her sister, Mrs Percy Anderson of Moor Lane, she says her husband lost his right eye but the doctor says left eye will be OK. He was a Bradford cloth designer and, before that, was employed by Messrs. J Knox & Son Ltd, Steeton (IG)
3 July	Isaac Grey, a native of Addingham and now residing in Bradford, received information, from the International Red Cross Society, that his son Corporal Maurice Grey, who was reported missing in March 1942, is now a PoW. Aged 24, he had served in the Royal Army Service Corps for 4 years, 3 of which were in Hong Kong. Grandparents, the late Mr and Mrs Isaac Grey, were well known in the village (CH)
3 July	Gunner Alfred Readshaw, aged 22, is missing in the Middle East. He, and parents Mr and Mrs Arthur Readshaw, live in Stockinger Lane. He joined up in 1940. A very good footballer and athlete, he had been a gardener in Ilkley. His brother Leslie, served on a Naval drifter (IG)
	Sergeant Eric Mason, in the Middle East, wrote a letter to the Knitting Circle: *'woollens very good in cold winters, sandstorms, and in the West Desert; are as precious as gold. Merciless sun and sand make the eyes sore'*. He had seen Addingham man Bernard Bester going through Alexandria on a lorry, but, even though he shouted, could not attract Bester's attention. He also met Tom Lancaster, another Addingham man. Pre-1939, Mason was an instructor with Athletic Club and a member at Cricket Club, Ilkley, British Legion, and Addingham Association Football Club (IG)
10 July	Gunner Readshaw is a PoW (IG)
	School meals: 100 to 120 pupils are hopeful to be provided with a kitchen site for school meals near High Council School, before the winter starts (CH)
17 July	Bill Bowes is reported missing. Pre-1939, Lieutenant Bowes was a partner in the business W E Bowes (Yorkshire) Ltd, insurance brokers, estate agents and business consultants, with offices at Otley and Ilkley. He was more widely known

News in Wartime

	as a Yorkshire and England cricketer (IG)
	174 men and 6 women are receiving comforts from the Knitting Circle (CH)
24 July	Private James Rishworth, aged 23, husband of Mrs P J Rishworth, Weston Road, and youngest son of Mr and Mrs Thomas Rishworth, Victoria Terrace, reported missing in Tobruk. He was on the staff at Scalebor Park Hospital pre-1939 and with the RAMC for two years. Posted overseas two years ago (IG)
	A lorry laden with toffee crashes in Addingham, by the Sailor Hotel. Contents were thrown over roadway and picked over by adults and children. In 1939 a lorry from the same firm crashed and free sweets for all was the result! (IG)
	Gunner Readshaw, in a letter home from PoW camp: *'fit and well, not wounded and decent food. Received a Red Cross parcel and can write once a week. Still practice physical training'*. Prior to the war he was the Athletic Club's outstanding member (IG)
31 July	Willie Foster dies of wounds in the Middle East. *(see Chapter 3)* (IG)
7 August	Readshaw's parents *(see 3 July)* received three letters, from Sheffield, Chipperfield (Herts), and London (Catholic Times), to say that their son's name was broadcast on Vatican Radio, that he was a PoW. All in Readshaw's camp (991128, Camp 66, Military Post 3400 Italy) say they are well treated and appreciated parcels, sent through Red Cross, of warm winter clothing, books, toilet articles etc. (IG)
	Evensong, at Addingham Parish Church, offered prayers for Trooper Willie Foster, who is the first war casualty from parish (CH) *(see 31 July above)*
14 August	Parish Council discussed the possibility of street savings groups in the village (IG)
	L.A.C William Henry Conyers (RAF), only son of Mr J Reeve Conyers of Morecambe and Ilkley, dies in Calcutta. Grandson of the late William Henry Conyers, he formerly played a leading part in charitable enterprises in the Ilkley area. Conyers' father played hockey for Ben Rhydding and Yorkshire. Educated at Pannal Ash College he entered Accountant General Office, Customs and Excise, Civil Service and, from there, the RAF (IG)
	Addingham Girl Guides to create a mile of books to raise money for the War effort (IG)

	Addingham woman drowns in River Wharfe. She was a school teacher in Bradford. Her body was found at Low Mill Dam but the incident happened at The Strid (IG) Parish Council decided to write to local corn merchants inviting tenders for the purchase of 3½ acres of oats grown on Council owned land (CH)
21 August	Bradford man travelled in a trade van to fish in Addingham: illegal use of car and petrol (IG)
21 August	Leonard Buckle, aged 14, takes leading part in athletic sports at school in Silsden and wins many prizes (IG) Addingham Ladies' Cricket Club held successful whist drive (CH)
11 September	Geoff Oddy is in hospital suffering from wounds received in enemy action *(See Chapter 3)* (IG) Day of National Prayer: a collection on behalf of the Soldiers, Sailors and Airmen's Families Fund realised £4/12/4d (IG) Knitting Circle Committee thanked George Dickson for gifts. Circle agreed to send 10/-, for a Christmas gift, to each Addingham man serving abroad (IG)
18 September	Herbert Holmes, a noted Addingham Cricketer, dies in the Coronation Hospital, aged 37. He was chief groundsman at Ermysteds Grammar School (IG) T Brear replaces the late Dr W Crabtree as Chairman, Addingham Parish Council (IG)
25 September	John W Holmes, aged 19, Merchant Navy Officer, torpedoed on his first voyage. Formerly an estate agent with Inghams in Ilkley, he writes: *'On a large cargo vessel since October 1941 and on 9 months tour duty. Torpedoed after lunch and immediately took to the boats and picked up after 2 hours by an old converted US coastguard cutter. Our ship not sunk but kept afloat by its cargo. I went back on to her, with others, but it was clear she was doomed – soon broke up after I left again and sank one day later. Submarines hunt in packs. Forbidden from throwing things overboard, should they leave a trail, which allows an enemy sub to follow a convoy'* (IG)
9 October	Youth Group to find a new home in Addingham. Original home needed for other war work (IG)
16 October	Gunner John Melville killed in the Middle East *(See Chapter 3)* (IG)
30 October	National Certificate in Electrical Engineering awarded to Leading Aircraftsman Walter Midwood, of Moor Lane, who

	joined the RAF 17 weeks ago with a view to becoming a pilot. A student at Bradford Technology College, he was employed by Wm Whitaker, Moor Lane (IG)
6 November	Raymond Sugden wrote to the Knitting Circle to say that there are 26 persons in his hut and he was the only one provided with woollies as extra comforts (IG)
13 November	Mr John England of Addingham: over 50 years a chorister; five years with Ilkley Parish Church choir and the remaining years at Addingham Parish Church (IG)
	Council agreed to hold an effort for Lady Cripps' Aid to China Fund (CH)
	Three Addingham schoolgirls raised £1 for the Red Cross PoW fund. They gave 2 concerts (CH)
20 November	Leading Aircraftman Jack Bradley and Sergeant E Mason, both of the Athletic Club, met in the Middle East – *'both keeping up fitness'*. Sergeant Mason was a salesman and Bradley was in textile engineering (IG)
4 December	Ilkley lady gets thanks from Russian Ambassador, Mr Maisky, for sending donation of £137/1/2d to Stalingrad Fund at the Embassy in London (IG)
11 December	£9/7/6d sent by Addingham ladies to Red Cross PoW Fund (IG)
18 December	Knitting Circle: George Dickson sent gifts, gratefully acknowledged (IG)
	Small toys sold for war effort (CH)

1943

1 January	Over 200 Addingham men and women in services but Christmas was kept in a pleasant and confident manner (IG)
	Knitting Circle: Out of 205 men and women serving in the Forces, only the addresses of eleven personnel had not been handed in (CH)
15 January	Parish Council discussion about bus stops in village (IG)
	Knitting Circle sent 42 10/- postal orders overseas and at home, 138 5/- postal orders and 138 pairs of socks (IG)
	Parish Council meeting: Compliments over reorganised system of bus stops (CH)

22 January	Intimation has been received by Mrs Riley of Aldersley Avenue, Skipton, that her husband, Private Sidney Riley of Skipton (formerly of Addingham) has died of wounds in India. Private Riley was 38 years of age and before the war was employed at Belle Vue Mills Skipton. He joined the Territorials before the war, and when war was declared he was called up immediately. He was in France and India and was wounded in Burma in Feb.1941. He leaves his wife, a hairdresser in Addingham, and one son (CH)
29 January	Red Cross effort: whist drive and supper raised £42/10s (IG) Knitting group raised £54/9s to provide home comforts (IG) A large number of appreciative letters have been received by the Knitting Circle from men and women serving in the forces in Canada, Malta, Gibraltar and the UK. They gave interesting accounts of their writers' experiences at Christmas (CH)
5 February	Rev Arthur Lumley, Addingham Methodist minister for two and a half years, is leaving the Methodist ministry and is to accept ordination in the Anglican Communion. He is widely respected in village (IG) Mr Lewis Steel, a well-known local farmer, is knocked over by a cyclist in Turner Lane and conveyed to Coronation Hospital with injuries to head, rib, and collar bone (IG) The PoW effort was dealt with in an address to members of Parish Church Mothers' Union (CH)
12 February	Parish Council: local public are not keen on the idea for a community feeding centre in village (IG) A recent whist drive raised £42/10s for the British Red Cross Society and Order of St John (CH)
12 February	85 gifts of 2/6d each have been sent to old pupils in the forces who attended the High School. This cash came from a concert. Appreciation letters received from all parts of the world (CH)
19 February	Addingham men meet up in the Middle East: Lance Sergeant John Thompson, Royal Artillery, writes to wife and four kids, in Moor Lane: *'Met old school mate Ernest Roe. Quite a lot of men from local area here'*. Sapper Gordon Beck says he met Norman Wall. Aircraftsman Tom Lancaster, in a letter to his sister in Moor Lane, visited Eric Mason, who has facial trouble, in hospital, but Mason is making a quick recovery. Another former Addingham boy, who now resides in Ilkley, is James

News in Wartime

	Willoughby – associated with the Athletic Club (IG)
19 February	Lister's Magazine, for Lister & Co employees: current issue on retirement refers to Mrs J Gill, High Mill Lane, who retired from Burnside Mill in October 1942 after 50 years as a 'gasser' *(A person who applied gas flame to finished cotton threads to smooth them - Ed)* and cleaner working in the gassing room. Now gassing frames are gone and old workers found it trying and unpleasant to tackle other work. She lived at Marchup and started work at age 10, hours of work 6.30am until late at night, wore clogs and a shawl. Her mother is 90 and one of Addingham's oldest people (IG)
26 February	Addingham man's sea experiences: Able Seaman R Emmott of Moor Lane, was away for 6 months, covered 80,000 miles, received no mail, spent one month in various parts and the rest at sea. He has experienced extremes heat and cold *('ice on deck 2 inches thick and often the convoy has had to scatter')*. Formerly keen member Athletic Club (IG)
5 March	Mrs Johnson (née Margaret Hargreaves) has raised £2/12s for the Red Cross through the sale of two lemons, sent to her from her husband serving in North Africa (IG)
12 March	Fire Service treatment: Parish Council discussed a letter from Divisional NFS giving telephone instructions in case of fire in the village. They seemed to lose sight of fact that they have a brigade of their own in Addingham (IG)
19 March	Lance Bombardier Thomas (Tommy) Perkins, Royal Artillery killed in North Africa (IG)*(see Chapter 3)*
26 March	Ilkley boys walking on Moor were burned by a mustard gas canister which they inadvertently picked up. They came out in burns/blisters on arms, legs, body, and in the eyes (IG) Gift from Mr George Dickson acknowledged by the Knitting Circle (CH)
2 April	Ratepayers meeting in Addingham: Anger expressed at a reduction in the number of bus stops in the village, particularly in the Moor Lane area. Also suggested that a sum of £309-12-6d is in-hand for lighting expenses and some form of modified street lighting for next winter (IG)
9 April	Plot of land secured to build small kitchen unit etc. for up to 140 Addingham school children, for their midday meals. Meals to be on a cash & carry basis (CH)
16 April	Aid to Russia fund: Football match between Athletic Club

	and Silsden Cadets (IG) Addingham Parish Council: Addingham's target to be £2,800, or about £1 per head of population, during 'Wings for Victory' week in May (CH) A new vehicle provided by National Fire Service for use in towing the village trailer pump (CH) Parish Council to tell Rural Council that it is in favour of a Youth Movement, if it is properly organised (CH)
23 April	Tom Lancaster, secretary of the Athletic Club, received letter from A/C Tom Lancaster, former Hon Treasurer, in the Middle East: *'Travelled widely but never seen anything as beautiful as Wharfedale'* (IG) NFU local grown: whist drive raised £18/2/11d and a ploughing competition raised £23/4/9d. To be distributed among local charities (CH)
7 May	Signalman W Millman is now a prisoner in a Taiwan camp. His wife, who lives in Lodge Hill, received a message which reported him missing at Singapore. He has been in the services 3 years and 12 years abroad. Employed by Messrs. Innes, Wells Road, as an electrician. His friend Alfred Houghton, a Cricket Club player, is also a prisoner in the same camp (IG) Addingham School attendance returns: High Council 84.21% Church of England 83.67% (IG)
14 May	Both small and large threshing machines are to be available this year, for Addingham and Ilkley farmers – mentioned at local N.F.U meeting (IG) Three members of Ilkley Home Guard suffered injuries received in bombing practice on moors north-west of Ilkley. They were taken to High Royds Hospital in Menston to receive treatment (IG)
21 May	Knitting Circle sent congratulations to Mrs Walter Millman and Mrs Ernest Turnpenny on news that their husbands were PoWs after being so long reported as missing (IG) *(see Chapter 3)* 'Wings for Victory', 22 May to 29 May: garden party at Hallcroft and open-air cinema show, many social events/whist drives (IG)
4 June	Lieutenant D W Potts, officer in Addingham Home Guard who is leaving to join forces, was given a gift at a social gathering at the Craven Heifer (CH)

News in Wartime

11 June	£40 will accrue as a result of performances of an entertaining variety show held in Addingham on Friday and Saturday evenings last week (CH)
	Two more Addingham schoolgirls have, this time, raised £10/5s by the sale of various small items given by friends (CH)
2 July	Miss Kathleen Brear and Flight Sergeant M C Rayner marry at the Parish Church (CH)
9 July	Slow progress over Addingham schools' canteen (IG)
16 July	Mrs Walter Millman received a postcard from her husband, Lance Corporal Millman, Royal Corps of Signals, in Japanese hands: *'health usual and working for pay'*.
	Mrs Turnpenny received a postcard saying that her husband *'is in Japanese hands and fit and well'* (this was probably sent by the International Red Cross) (IG)
	Sergeant Navigator James Townson met Jimmy Rishworth and Ken Horsman, of Addingham, and hopes to meet other Addingham men later (IG)
	Marine Ken Hargreaves, in India, says he was confronted by a cobra, but an officer shot it (IG)
	Help for forces from companies of two of licensed houses in the village: The Crown raised £15 for the Knitting Circle and The Swan £5/1/6d (CH)
6 August	Addingham man in Japanese hands: Musician Hedley Adams was on HMS Exeter when sunk but survived to be a prisoner. HMS Exeter was one of three ships which cornered the German pocket battleship Graf Spee at the Battle of the River Plate in December 1939 and forced the German ship into Montevideo harbour in Uruguay where she was scuttled. The Exeter was sunk south of Borneo, on 1 March 1942, by the Japanese cruisers Nachi and Haguro, and a torpedo from the Japanese destroyer Inazuma.
	Hedley was a worker at his father's Barcroft Shed and an accomplished musician, well-known in local music circles. Father is in business as dress goods manufacturer, a member of the Parish Council and Chairman of the Memorial Close Committee (IG)
	Gunner Townson, son of Mr and Mrs Alf Townson, Southfield Terrace, is in the Middle East and met another Addingham man, Frank Smith, formerly employed by John Ridley & Son contractors: *'Smith still the same, full of fun'*, said

Townson (IG)

For the first time in many years, Addingham mills closed together last week. Most people spent the holidays at home but there were no arrangements for extra attractions (IG)

20 August Hedley Adams has written to his parents, and broadcast on radio from Tokyo, 30 July 1943: *'Keeping well, longing for home. Give Joyce (his fiancée) fondest love – to you as well. Take care and don't worry'* (IG)

Leading Aircraftman Bernard Bester, son of Mr and Mrs P Bester, Low Mill, well-known Addingham cricketer and footballer, has been in hospital for three months, in the Middle East, suffering from 'desert disease' which has affected his hands. (IG)

Aid to Russia Fund rises to 38s in a recent collection. Raised by Addingham school children, and by Gerald Greenwood for Red Cross PoW Fund (IG)

27 August Joan Stapleton, Graham Southwell and Valerie Southwell raised 8/2d for Red Cross by means of a sale (IG)

3 September Addingham man, Roy Richardson, reported missing, *is now a PoW*. Others who are PoWs are Charlie Allan, Alfred Readshaw, Walter Millman and Ernest Turnpenny (IG)

Rev James Clegg, Methodist minister in Addingham, gave talk on 'Overseas to China' where he had spent the first 15 years of his work (IG)

10 September Members of the Knitting Circle and the Women's Voluntary Service received Certificate of Honour from Sir Archibald Sinclair in connection with Addingham's 'Wings for Victory' National Savings campaign for 1943. Money is invested in Defence Bonds (IG)

Addingham housing: Parish Council dissatisfied that request for 24 houses to be included in a building programme for the first year post-war was not granted by Skipton Rural Council, which proposed only 16 houses. Eventually, Addingham Parish Council agreed with the Rural Council decision (IG)

School canteen for Addingham to open on 20 September 1943 at High Council School. A cook and maid have been engaged and a Canteen Committee would be formed later (IG)

Knitting Circle: free wool is available to knit garments for the Russians (IG)

WVS invested £140 in 3% Defence Bonds as result of Addingham 'Wings for Victory' week (CH)

News in Wartime

24 September   In the 'book recovery', Addingham has collected 7,043 books weighing over 1½ tons. In addition, through teachers at Silsden Modern School persuading Addingham scholars there to take books to swell the Silsden drive, over 500 books were taken from Addingham to Silsden. Addingham broke the record in the Rural Area, during last book drive, by over 3 hundredweights. A very satisfactory situation (IG)

Christmas Gifts for the Troops: gifts acknowledged from, among others, Mrs George Dickson.

100 Addingham men and women are now serving overseas and they are to receive £1 each this Christmas, and the remainder of the 206 who are in the forces and who are stationed in various parts of this country, will receive 10s and a pair of socks (IG)

Warden Post: in future the Warden's attendance at Old School Post will be every Tuesday night, commencing 28 September, from 8.00pm to 9.30pm. Replacements and repairs to civilian respirators will be attended to only on these nights (IG)

24 September   Midday meals for schoolchildren will be a liberal helping of meat pie with 2 veg and sponge pudding and custard. *'Meal well cooked and appetising'* (CH)

1 October   Third Engineer J. M. Heap is home in Ilkley after 74 days in an open boat when his tanker was sunk by the enemy in the Indian Ocean. He was one of only seven survivors. He was later associated with The Fleece in Addingham.

8 October   Knitting Circle: Names of Addingham men and women serving in forces coming in too slowly, especially in view of fact that the time for sending Christmas parcels is now rapidly diminishing (IG)

15 October   Parish Council is still refusing to accept, without further protest, the decision of Skipton R.C to reduce the number of houses to be erected in Addingham under the Post-War Housing Scheme, from 24 to 16 (IG)

Mrs Sarah Ann Foster, 6 High Mill Lane, celebrated her 90th birthday. She has been a widow for 41 years, has 17 children, 6 of whom are living, 10 grandchildren, and 7 great-grandchildren. She lost her youngest son, Tom, in the last war and a grandson, Willie Foster, in the present war. She is the oldest inhabitant of the village and has lived at present address for 54 years. Her only sister is 80 years old (IG)

22 October	Farmers protest to West Riding War Agriculture Committee with regard to the condition of Straight Lane, Addingham Moorside. The Committee said that fair wear and tear was the cause rather than the continuous travelling of their machinery over its surface (one report was of a spiked harrow being dragged down the road) (IG) Warning is also given that farmers delivering their own milk, owing to shortage of staff, might find their registration category would have to be altered (IG) Helping the Red Cross: An Addingham lady raised a £5 sum by knitting for her Ilkley Red Cross Committee friends (IG) Knitting Circle welcomed a visit from Chief Petty Officer Eric Dickinson, home on leave after spending nearly 2 years in West Africa (IG) Local man on wireless: Donald Merritt of Addingham, who is serving with RAF in India, broadcast to his parents, Mr and Mrs Bradley, 2 Kitty Fold, in 'India Calling' on Sunday morning. Pre-war he was employed by Messrs. Bolton Emmott, Cockroft & Co Ltd, Wolsey Shed, Main Street (CH)
29 October	Sergeant Navigator James Townson, the eldest son of Mr and Mrs William Townson, Southfield Terrace, joined the Forces in February 1943 and trained to be an officer in Southern England. He is now in India with the RAF but is in hospital with dysentery. *'Appalled by squalor and poverty and the huge gap between rich and poor in India'.* He was at Ilkley Grammar School, then worked at Ilkley Public Library. (IG)
5 November	Gunner Harold McQuade (R.A.) is in hospital in Italy suffering from wounds. Was at Dunkirk and since has served in North Africa (IG) Sergeant Air Gunner Wallace Bruce, formerly employed as a porter at Addingham Rail Station, is believed to have lost his life in air operations. His mother, in Skipton, has been told. Aged 22, been on 11 ops. with RAF since November 1941. In earlier days, he assisted Charlie Duckett in organising dances for Addingham men in the services (IG)
11 November	Mr E Benson dies aged 63 at Moor Lane. His parents live at Brockabank Farm. Served in First World War and was a PoW for 18 months (IG)
12 November	Parish Council: Addingham is the only parish to have its promise of housing reduced – in this case from 24 to 16 (IG)
19 November	Addingham man home on leave: Gunner Frank Smith, son of

News in Wartime

Mrs Nathanial Smith, Rose Terrace. In Army 3 years, 38 years old, he was a nurseryman working in Guiseley. Wounded at El Alamein and later fought in Tunisia and Sicily. He heard of the death of his cousin, the late Trooper T Bolton Wilkinson, an Addingham man of 8 years standing, living in Ilkley pre-war. Smith had no idea he was so near his cousin and actually saw the crash of the tank that he was in (IG)

26 November Bring and buy sale raises £36 for District Nursing (IG)

3 December Private J Rishworth, Victoria Terrace, transferred to a German prison camp (had been in Italian hands since Tobruk surrender in 1942). Had been with R.A.M.C. 2 years 4 months before being captured. With him in German camp are Gunner A. Readshaw, son of Mr and Mrs Arthur Readshaw, 10 Rose Terrace, and Ken Wheater who lived many years in Ilkley (IG)

3 December *'Excellent work being done by the Knitting Circle'* – stressed at the annual meeting held in Conservative Club. Very grateful for all knitters and generous financial contributions (IG)

Skipton MP since 1933, George William Rickards dies aged 66. A silk spinner in Skipton, he had a long association with Conservatives and was a member of many Craven organisations. A serious and conscientious MP (CH)

10 December Gunner Frank Dean (RA), only son of Mrs Dean and the late Mr Charles Dean, Low Mill, mentioned in dispatches. Aged 29, in Army 3½ years and, pre-1939, worked at Lister's Mill in Addingham. *'A gunner is a dispatch rider who carries messages cheerfully and willingly through shellfire'* (IG)

No further collections to be made, nationally, of tins, bottles, and jars, owing to large accumulations built up throughout the country. All other forms of salvage are still very urgently wanted, the demand is great as ever. Addingham is a leading place in the Rural Council's list for salvage collection (IG)

17 December A good year for the NFU (Addingham & Ilkley branch). Membership was 74 and now has paid up membership of 90 – just in one year (IG)

Writing from one of HM ships, Arthur Turnpenny says that wherever he has been he has *'yearned for a sight of the Moor and prepared to exchange all pleasures to be found in other parts of the world for the chance of a few peaceful hours in the Dales. A word from home counts for more than the result of a battle on the other side of the world'* (IG)

Short sharp election campaign for Skipton seat: polling day 7

	January 1944 (CH)
24 December	Readshaw is in same German prison camp as Rishworth and *'they talk for hours on a night'*, says Readshaw in a letter to his parents (IG)
31 December	Mr Whitham, head of local tailors and outfitters business, dies on Christmas Eve aged 61 (IG)

1944

7 January	Addingham Varieties raise money (over £80) which will eclipse that raised by them in 'Wings for Victory' week – this money raised, by the men and ladies at four concerts, will go to the Addingham Post-War Memorial Fund. Addingham Varieties appeared with The Variety Girls and Jimmie's Juveniles (IG)
14 January	Two Addingham schoolgirls raise £25/10s on behalf of Duke of Gloucester's Red Cross Fund (IG)
	Knitting Circle in the 'Raise the Standard and Army Campaign'. They set their target at £700, which they have easily exceeded by collecting £982/17/6d. They are also preparing an after-the-war Memorial Fund (IG)
	Common Wealth Party (nowadays an obsolete term 'for the general good or public welfare') unexpectedly wins Skipton election, in some part due to farmer's dissatisfaction in the division at Ministry of Agriculture policies, as applied to the Craven district. Basically, the farmers defected. Hugh Lawson (Common Wealth) 12,222, (Lawson was an Army Lieutenant released from his military duty to sit in Parliament), Harry Riddihough (Conservative) 12,001 and Joseph Toole (Independent) 3,029. Common Wealth majority of 221. The poll represented upwards of 70% of registered voters (CH)
21 January	As result of success of concerts during 'Wings Week', more are to be held in village to raise funds (CH)
28 January	Up to date: Knitting Circle told that 102 letters have been received from Addingham men and women in Service, acknowledging their Christmas gifts (IG)
	Receipts for the year from street savings group have realised £3,669/10/5d. This sum is apart from the £23,000 during 'Wings for Victory Week' (CH)
4 February	One of most successful whist drives and dances ever held in

the village was organised by the Addingham Combined Civil Defence Services. The receipts, and number of local charities which will benefit, is to be announced later (IG)

Churchill thought a victory for Common Wealth in the Brighton and Hove by-election, as in Skipton by-election, would strike an unsettling blow at those on whom falls the task of bringing the country back to safety and peace. *'A man may feel, with perfect sincerity, that it is his duty to strike such a blow, but he should have the sense to perceive what he is doing and the candour to avow it'* (CH)

11 February — Children's Concert Party raises £25 for Red Cross PoW Fund (IG)

Civil Defence Exercise in Addingham: Air Raid Precaution personnel, the Home Guard Bomb Disposal Unit and representatives from local fire services all combined in a Civil Defence exercise in Addingham on 6 February. The whole exercise arranged by Sergeant A M Cowan of the Auxiliary Bomb Disposal Unit (IG)

18 February — Sergeant Bester, who has 'desert hands', is returning to the UK from the Middle East, where it is hoped his hands will be OK soon (IG)

Lieutenant Sergeant J Thomson mentioned in dispatches for 'gallant and distinguished services'. Has been in army 2½ years and served overseas 18 months. Went through the Sicilian campaign. Employed by Messrs. George Rishworth and Sons, contractors, Ilkley (IG)

Vera Shackleton and Brenda Robinson, both schoolgirls, have sent £6 to Mrs Churchill's Aid to Russia appeal. This is their second donation (the first raised £5) (IG)

25 February — New PAYE tax scheme, which is about to become law, was explained to NFU (Addingham & Ilkley) members: successful working depends on employers and employees (CH)

3 March — New MP, in a speech, says, *'in Armed Services today, there is a great desire, among young people, for progressive ideas in politics. A Common Wealth must take such actions as to ensure that the fruits of victory are not lost'* (CH)

17 March — House of Commons rebuke for Skipton's MP: *'alleged encouragement to serving personnel to commit acts of indiscipline'* (CH)

Agreed to fix 'Salute the Soldier' week from 22 to 29 April, with a target of £250,000 (CH)

Ilkley branch of Common Wealth organised a meeting, held

	at Addingham, with a view to forming a branch. Chairman Mrs Bradley and Vice Chairman Mr C F Wall (CH)
31 March	Mrs Agnes Mason died in her 69th year. She lived at Reynard Ing, Addingham **(see photo below)**. Her husband died years earlier and she carried on farming with the help of her son Thomas.

6 April	As part of 'Salute the Soldier' week, the Home Guard, on 23 April, are to give a weapon display (IG)
21 April	Aircraftman Bester is now in the UK with hand skin disease (IG)
Kenneth Hargreaves, home on leave after 3 years overseas, has seen service in Middle East theatre of war and India. Aged 23, he worked at Ilkley and Bingley post offices (IG)
Mrs Egan, of Bolton Road, received intimation that her only son, in RAF and serving in India Command, is missing (CH)
Aircraftsman Bernard Bester has been invalided home from Middle East suffering from eczema (CH)
Kenneth Hargreaves, in India, had an alarming encounter with a cobra but, luckily, leapt out of open window before the snake attacked (CH)
28 April	Walter Midwood, only son of Mr and Mrs Alfred Midwood, promoted to Pilot Officer in RAF, passing out in Canada where he has been stationed since last September. Active in Scouts and, indeed, a King's Scout, he was employed as electrician by William Whitaker in Moor Lane (IG)
Private Joe Hilbeck, only son of James Hilbeck, Fleece Hotel, is home on leave from the Pioneer Corps (IG)

News in Wartime

	Talk on Old Age Pensions given by Tom Wilkinson, Secretary of Keighley branch, OAP Federation (IG)
	The Addingham branch of the Common Wealth party is requesting Parliament to investigate pensions, at £1 per week at age 60 (IG)
	'Salute the Soldier': exhibition of photos of many Addingham men and women. Village target £3,500 and, at opening ceremony, a figure of £4,000 was marked on the indicator (CH)
12 May	Addingham's new houses saga rumbles on. Parish Council suggested 4 possible sites but the Ministry of Health only 2 of them, and they turned both down. Concern also expressed of the slowness of emptying ashbins (IG)
	Nursing Association's 22nd AGM held. The Nurse had paid 2,621 visits comprising of 1,245 general, 128 maternity, 244 midwifery, 242 ante-natal, 484 infant health, 44 school and 234 casual (IG)
26 May	Anton Wynn, of Southfield Terrace, died aged 52. He served in last war with the 6th Dukes and was wounded in the leg, leaving him with a limp (IG)
2 June	Cottages sold: 5 stone built cottages, numbers 1 to 5 Daisy Hill, sold by auction at Sailor Hotel, on Friday, by Dacre Son & Hartley, for £810 (IG)
	Mr James Harrison, Meadowbank, Southfield, local chemist in village for many years, dies; (IG)
	Mr J F Atack re-elected Chair, Education Committee (IG)
	Average school attendance in Addingham during the previous month was 92.03% and this was the best in the Otley education district (IG)
	Classes for keep fit, country dancing and dressmaking to be held in academic year 1944/5 (IG)
	Knitting Circle's social efforts during 'Salute the Soldier' week raised £189/5/11d (CH)
16 June	Addingham branch meeting of the Common Wealth party held. Mrs Hugh Lawson, the wife of MP for the area, outlined the history of the party, dating back to 1942 when it fused with Forward March. It was created post-Munich, in 1938. The object was a vital democracy and common ownership and they hoped that at some time in the future the voters would have an opportunity of a straight vote on common ownership. The land, after Parliamentary approval, would then be owned by the people (IG)

Addingham in World War Two

20 June — Knitting Circle members reported a falling off in savings and they made an appeal for savings at this critical stage in the war (CH)

7 July — Mrs Perkins, whose son Tom died 12 months ago in North Africa, has received a letter from Lance Bombardier Earle of Ilkley (IG)

Youth Council is still trying to procure a suitable building. In the meantime, young people get together to organise concerts, dances, whist drives and sports to add to the fund for a new building (IG)

14 July — The Station Chaplain, Flight Lieutenant A B Simpson, writes to Mr and Mrs Charlie Newton, Moor Lane, about their only son, killed in flying accident in Canada. (CH)

Gunner Gaythorne Kettlewell, whose wife resides at Victoria Terrace, met up with another Addingham man in Normandy, namely Allan Mason. Mason also thought he had seen Jack Smith in Normandy, but could not be certain (CH)

Captain G B Drayson met Conservative workers after being adopted as Tory candidate for the Division, in September (he was later MP, 1945 to 1974) (CH)

21 July — Sapper E. W. Potts, Moor Lane, aged 36, only son of Mr and Mrs W. Potts, Dean Street, Ilkley, commissioned into Pioneer Corps. A builder/contractor in Addingham, Mr Potts was called up July 1943 and joined the Royal Engineers, then transferred to the Pioneer Corps. Before being called up he held a commission in Addingham Home Guard (IG)

28 July — All mills closed in Addingham during holiday week and many people spent the holiday away from home (IG)

4 August — Three lots offered for sale in village by auction were withdrawn: 32, 34, 36, 38 Main Street, 1, 2, 3, 4 Cockshott Place and cottages 4, 6, 12, 14 School Lane (IG)

Education Committee: 3,430 midday meals provided from school canteen during July (IG)

11 August — Three Addingham men meet: 2 of 3 sons of Mr and Mrs Ted Hudson, of Cockshott Place, are in Burma and have met. The other brother Dick is in France. Father was in Boer War and First World War (IG)

1 September — Bombardier Jack Perkins, Druggist Lane, is making steady progress in a Glasgow Hospital after being wounded in the left shoulder while serving in France. His younger brother, Tommy Perkins, was killed in March 1944. He was one of

News in Wartime

	four members of family serving in Forces (IG)
	Miss K Allsopp, Common Wealth Party organiser for Yorkshire, addressed members of the Addingham Branch of Common Wealth on election organisation (IG)
8 September	Lance Corporal Lowcock wounded in India, serving with Military Blue in India Command. He is in hospital awaiting a third operation after being hit by shrapnel. Aged 36 and, pre-war, a gardener at Nesfield, he played cricket for Bolton Abbey and Addingham. His brother, Lance Corporal L Lowcock, is serving in the Tank Corps in France (IG)
	Addingham Education Committee: 2nd place in Otley area for Addingham in terms of school attendance. Addingham High School 87.09%; Addingham C of E 92.10%. 3,430 school meals served during the month (IG)
15 September	Mr and Mrs Oddy, Farfield, received information that their youngest son, Leading Motor Mechanic Oddy, has been killed. (IG) *(See Chapter 3)*
	Parish Council: concern over bridge leading to the Garth, adjoining the Manor House (IG)
	Special machine for grain drying, in use at Addingham, works in conjunction with combined harvesters. Dryers take out excess moisture and prevent grain going musty in granaries. Grain has to be threshed before ready for dryer (IG)
22 September	Battle of Britain service took the form of tributes, at Parish Church, to those men who gave lives for the country. It had brought war to turning point and a better and purer world when peace comes (IG)
	Addingham street lighting: Parish Council told that there were 80 to 90 lamps and asked how many more are required in the main thoroughfare? Agreed to ask for a further 6 lamps for the time being (IG)
13 October	Lance Corporal Fred Hartley has written to his mother in Moor Lane to say, *'Run into by lorry and suffered a broken ankle and big toe, but progressing favourably'*. They have four sons in forces and two are also overseas. Fred joined up before war and went to France, about D-Day (IG)
	Corporal Stanley Fisher, Wesley Place, wounded by a shell exploding near him in Belgium. Doing well now and *'excellent food in hospital'*. Had a visit from well-known GB stage and screen stars. *'Prices of foodstuff in Belgium very high but Belgians are very friendly people'*. He is aged 35 and has 2 young children. Joined up April 1942 and sent to France after D-Day. Pre-

Addingham in World War Two

	war, was at Lister & Co, Low Mill. A well-known footballer, he played football and cricket for Addingham. Brother, Fred, well-known member of Ilkley Rugby Club, was killed in First World War (IG) Civil defence talk on chemical warfare (IG)
20 October	Timothy Brear, of Moor Lane, dies aged 70. For many years he played an active part in public life in the village, in which he lived all his life. He was a timber merchant at William Brear & Sons and a keen cricketer (CH) ***(See photo below)*** House to house collection for Christmas Fund raised £92/2/6d (CH)
27 October	Sapper H P Wall RE killed in NW Europe (IG) *(see Chapter 3)* William Turnpenny, Main Street, a signalman at Ben Rhydding, injured in road accident on 26 October. He was cycling along the main road to work and, near Cocking (Cocken) End, he collided with a motorcyclist. Taken to Coronation Hospital and Leeds Infirmary with a compound fracture of the right arm and shock (IG)

Timothy Brear (extreme right) with his 5 brothers at the sawmill before the war (see 20 October)

3 November	The Home Guard was stood down from Wednesday 1 November this week and will remain in reserve until disbanded – an official War Office announcement (CH)
17 November	Parish Council unanimous in the desire for a children's clinic in the village. 120 children in village needed a clinic and currently had to go to Ilkley or Skipton (IG) Bicentenary of the coming of Methodism to Addingham. (CH)

News in Wartime

	Two Addingham schoolboys, aged 13, each fined 10s and ordered to pay damages/costs of 15/9d for damaging a walnut tree (CH)
	Poppy Day appeal raised £43/4s
24 November	Talk on sheep dogs to members of Addingham/Ilkley Young Farmers' Club (IG)
8 December	Education matters: attendance returns seriously affected by children's ailments (CH)
15 December	Parish Council told news that, due to war conditions, it is not possible for Addingham to have a clinic. Issue of post-war housing raised, and, when new road begins, 8 houses would have to come down (IG)
	Knitting Circle received letter from WVS HQ appealing for household goods to help those who had lost their homes (IG)
22 December	Bomb Disposal Squad: Mr A M Cowen of Addingham had received a letter from Ministry of Aircraft Production to say, *'Not now considered necessary to maintain the Bomb Disposal Sub-Unit'* of which he had been in charge (IG)
	NFU (Addingham & Ilkley branch) meeting, 20 December 1944, with reference to post-war planning. A letter sent to Ilkley Urban Council suggesting the road from Heber's Ghyll be continued along the Moorside to join Straight Lane. Dissatisfaction expressed about lateness of cultivation of arable land in Addingham district; lecturers had visited NFU to give sound advice on dealing with the situation (CH)
29 December	School parties: praise heaped on school canteen staff in village for providing such splendid meals, day by day (IG)

1945

5 January	Knitting Circle currently knitting comforts for bombed-out children (CH)
12 January	Private Jack Stapleton dies (IG) *(see Chapter 3)*
	Knitting Circle faith tea: Poor attendance of adults, and pointed out that public would have to give greater support if they wished to encourage idea of a village hall in post-war years (IG)
19 January	Mr D Storey, Bolton Road, had received a letter from his son

Trooper Fred Storey, Westminster Dragoons, to say he is in a Worcester hospital. His left leg *'knocked about a bit when a wall came down in Germany'*. He came to England, via Brussels, by plane and, hopefully, will be moved to Yorkshire later. Aged 21 and joined up at 18. Landed on D-Day. Employed by Messrs. Carr & Co at their Addingham grocery branch (IG)

26 January — Common Wealth Party at Addingham: The Common Wealth MP for Skipton, Hugh Lawson, gave address on Greece (IG) Captain G B Drayson (later the Tory MP for Skipton) presented prizes at whist drive and dance – keen to meet those constituents who had relatives in the Forces. Keenly interested in wool, cotton and farming industries (IG)

9 February — School holidays in Addingham for 1945: Shrovetide 12 February, Easter 30 March to 9 April, Whitsuntide 21 May to 28 May, Summer 23 July to 20 August, mid-term 15 October to 22 October and Christmas 24 December to 7 January 1946 (IG)

16 February — Council heard about poor gas pressure on Moor Lane. Ilkley authority agreed to insert a main of wider diameter (CH)
Question of later buses between Keighley and Ilkley – currently the last one leaves at 9 pm (CH)

16 February — Private James Rishworth, RAMC, repatriated from German prison camp and now in a UK hospital. He had also been in an Italian camp since being captured in Tobruk in 1942. His father, Tom, lives in Victoria Terrace, but his mother has died. Aged 26, his wife lives in Ilkley. One of three serving brothers. Before joining up he was an attendant at Scalebor Park Hospital (CH)

23 February — Knitting Circle: Gift received from Mr George Dickson. Circle told that Miss Ettie Parling had joined the WRENS, the first woman from Addingham to join this branch of the service (IG)

9 March — Photo **(opposite)** of 'Addingham Varieties of 1945', produced by Jimmy Hadley. Grown-ups in picture are Mr E and Mrs Jean McNulty, Mr Jimmy Hadley, Mrs Bessie Greenwood and Mr Ken Wilde (IG)
Addingham plans for education: a plea for Ilkley merger. Hostility to schools going to Skipton Rural Area. A pledge

had been made that, when Senior School is built in Ilkley, the 11+ scholars at Addingham would be transferred to Ilkley. *'Honour that pledge'* (IG)

16 March	Parish Council agreed to give support to Education Sub-Committee request that Addingham is included with Ilkley, rather than becoming part of Craven Division at Skipton, under the new Education Act. *'The link with Ilkley is natural'* (IG)
16 March	Parish Council: Need to reinstate Moor Lane bus stop or give Addingham passengers preference on last buses out of Ilkley to Keighley and Skipton (CH)
29 March	Ratepayers meet at Addingham regarding the rates, already 13s 6d, going directly to the country (IG)
6 April	Final meeting of Education Sub-Committee (CH)
13 April	Private Scott, youngest son of Mr and Mrs Andrew Scott, Marchup, making cakes from captured Japanese flour and sugar at Meiktila in Burma! In March, after a lightning thrust across the Irrawaddy, they captured sugar, chocolates, flour and tea. Lakeside Canteen in Meiktila opened doors to British and Indian soldiers and officers. A 'Military Observer' comments: *Japanese tea is excellent and sugar equally good. Milkshakes are the alternative. Even Japanese sweets have been found. 42-gallon vats from a local brewery ensure a constant supply of tea. All cooking is done in an oven made of 2-gallon drums'.* Private Scott joined heavy AA battery in July 1940, was sent overseas in September 1941 and had been in India until recently, when he was sent to Burma. In civilian life a monumental mason (IG) War Memorial Fund: Sum of £44 raised by means of a whist drive, supper and dance organised in aid of Post-War Memorial Fund (IG)

20 April	Addingham man decorated: Mrs A. Hollingworth, 20, Low Mill Street, has received news that her son, Sergeant William Henry Hollingworth, aged 32, Royal Armoured Corps, has been awarded the Military Medal. In army for 7 years and serving in France for nearly a year. A PT instructor (IG) Addingham guardian: Dennis Clarke Milburn, aged 24, the older son of Mr and Mrs George Milburn, Church Street, has been killed in action on Western Front. (IG) *(See Chapter 3)* Hugh Lawson, Common Wealth MP for Skipton, to stand for West Harrow in London at the next election. He pledged, at a by-election in January 1944, that he would not stand in Skipton again if the Labour Party put up a candidate and he has kept his promise. He will start as a Common Wealth candidate at Harrow. Aged 33, born in Leeds, a civil engineer in various parts of UK, Army Volunteer October 1939 and called up May 1940. 2nd Lieutenant in Royal Engineers and to RAF Croydon during Battle of Britain. From October 1940 to May 1943 he served in the REs in Gibraltar. Then posted to Edinburgh and temporarily lost rank of Captain. His wife is a full-time munitions worker.(IG)
27 April	Public meeting held on 2 February to determine nature of Welcome Home events for Addingham returnees. At a similar event in Addingham in 1919, only 20% of service personnel from the village were present and only 24 attended this meeting. Mr E Holmes suggested forming a committee to get things moving. Unanimously decided to create both a fund and a committee (CH)
4 May	Addingham Nursing Association AGM: In the last year, District Nurse made 3,116 visits consisting of 1,667 general, 189 antenatal, 123 midwifery, 108 maternity, 802 health, 174 casual, 18 schools and 35 schoolchildren. 326 subscribers. 40 vouchers (7/6d each) from the Benevolent Fund distributed at Christmas (CH)
11 May	Victory whist drive and dance arranged by members of WVS, and Addingham Varieties Concert was held in National School on Tuesday. Offerings from Parish Church went to Christian Reconstruction in Europe (IG)
13 May	Throat sweets, wine and spirits were stolen from Addingham Goods Yard between 21 and 22 April. Penalties and costs totalling £59/6/7d imposed on Tom Ridley, bricklayer, of Victoria Terrace (CH) Parish Council told that a duplicate bus service would be

News in Wartime

	introduced for the benefit of Addingham people, but could not increase the number of bus stops (CH)
16 May	Trooper James Henry Woodfield, aged 24, killed in action in NW Europe. (IG) *(See Chapter 3)*
	'Welcome Home' plans for fundraising: house to house collection, bring and buy, a gala day with procession, sports, gymkhana and sheep dog trials (IG)
25 May	Returning PoWs: Private Charles Allan, captured at St Valery in June 1940, sent to Thorn in Poland. In 1945 he was on a forced march away from advancing Russians towards Americans. He praises Red Cross, Knitting Circle, and party held by former work mates at Low Mill. Was in Addingham Minor's football team.
	Gunner Readshaw, captured in Gazala, Libya in 1942 and remained in Italian hands for over a year until Italy surrendered, and then in German hands for 2 years. Sent to camp on Polish border and worked in a factory until RAF hit it. Then forestry work and forced march westwards. His fitness helped him through being PoW (CH)
	Collection at Parish Church recently raised £13/13s in aid of Christian Reconstruction in Europe Fund (CH)
9 June	New branch of Labour Party set up in village (CH)
22 June	Addingham Gala Day headed by Burley Band. The procession marched from The Green to the Cricket Field, kindly lent for the occasion by the Club. Large number of entries and judges had a hard task (IG)
	J P Davies, the Labour candidate at the General Election, addresses a meeting in the High Council School (IG)
29 June	Addingham 'Welcome Home': £200 raised by Remembrance Fund at a 'bring and buy' (CH)
	Members of Knitting Circle held their fortnightly meeting at Conservative Club on Tuesday 26 June when gifts were acknowledged from Mrs Holmes (Hallcroft), Mr and Mrs McNulty and Mr G Dickson (Coincidentally, Mr Dickson died on 29 June and the Knitting Circle's regrets were expressed at the death of a good supporter). (CH)
12 July	Parish Council told that Youth Council agreed to inaugurate a scheme for provision of a youth-hut – '*a vital amenity, also, for the whole village*' (CH)
13 July	Youth Hut for Addingham: Council agrees to postpone discussion until later (IG)

Addingham in World War Two

27 July
Mr Henman Demaine found dead from gunshot wounds, by a stream at the back of his house. He was a well-known and highly respected tradesman (IG)
Blood donors still needed in whole of West Yorkshire (CH)
Election: Captain Drayson wins narrow majority on 81% poll: G B Drayson (Conservative) 17,905, John Davis (Labour) 15,704, Lieutenant Colonel E. Townsend (Liberal) 9,546 (CH)

10 August
Horse races at Addingham: £300 for Welcome Home Fund (IG)
Addingham Salvationists, Major and Mrs Arthur J Wild, 15 Wesleyan Terrace, with lifelong experience in Salvation Army, each received a ribbon for the star, for services in France, 1939-1940. When Paris fell, they were in charge of a large canteen in St Malo, working round clock to care for troops and refugees of many nationalities. The canteen was in a cinema, with a large stock of food, and when Germans were only half an hour away they told people to help themselves and leave nothing for Germans. They had worked in East Africa and Keighley. Due to a mosquito bite leading to delayed shock, the Major was invalided out of the Army (IG)

17 August
Addingham parents angry when Education Minister decided to allow Addingham children to attend schools under Skipton's jurisdiction rather than Ilkley. To be raised at WRCC level – namely, a school in the village to keep all children at home (IG)
Mills closed for 2 days and a united service of thanksgiving was held at Parish Church (IG)

17 August
Mother and 3-year-old child drowned at Addingham on 16 August: Mrs Norah Emery and the child Francis. The child was dead when plucked from water at Low Mill and mother died later in hospital at Menston. Mrs Emery had been depressed and nervous and was under medical care but she had never threatened to take her own life (CH)

24 August
Many scenes of joyful celebration on Wednesday and Thursday, 15 August and 16 August for VE Day. Bonfires were lit and there was a large gathering on the village green for community singing and impromptu dancing. Village decked with flags and bunting. A special service held at Parish Church by Rev H D Blakeney Flynn on 15 August and a thanksgiving service on 19 August (CH)

News in Wartime

31 August	Victory party was held, for children aged 3 to 14 years of age, in the Low School, on 22 September (IG)
	Welcome Home Fund now standing at £880 (CH)
21 September	Addingham Savings Group has fixed its targets for Skipton District Thanksgiving Week at £2,000 or more (CH)
28 September	Lance Corporal Millman is safe in allied hands. Joined Royal Corps Signals February 1940 and sent overseas March 1941, a prisoner at Singapore in 1942. Prior to joining up, employed by Messrs Innes electricians, Wells Road, Ilkley (IG)
	Bandsman Adams safe in Australia, after three and a half years of hell. He was on HMS Exeter when sunk in the Java Sea in March 1942 and parents had no letter from him until the Australia letter posted 19 September 1945, but the BBC picked up Tokyo radio message in July 1943 to say he was a prisoner. News conveyed by Red Cross to his parents. Worked at Barcroft Mills pre-war (IG)
	An ardent worker for Knitting Circle and WVS, Sarah Shackleton dies aged 49. Wife of Harold Shackleton, grocer, of Main Street (IG)
5 October	Sergeant Roy Richardson, RAF, son of Mr J W Richardson of The Green, a PoW in Japan for 3½ years, writes home freely without being told what to write. In Sumatra jungle when he heard the news of the Japanese surrender. A flautist soloist in Skipton Permanent Orchestra. Has been heard on BBC (IG)
	Skipton's Common Wealth party is to continue, despite losing to the Conservatives in the General Election (CH)
19 October	RSPCA bronze medal to Victor Tiffany, son of Mrs Tiffany, Main Street, for rescuing pigs from a burning sty in the middle of the night (IG)
26 October	Addingham Male Voice Choir: varied programme of songs in Ben Rhydding Methodist Schoolroom (IG)
2 November	Darts and dominoes handicap raised £50/10s for 'Welcome Home & Remembrance' fund (CH)
9 November	Red Cross thanks Welfare and Social Department of SU Carburettor Co Ltd, Wharfedale Factory, Low Mill, for gifts of cash, sports gear, piano and books (IG)
	Victory bonfire held on field off Bolton Road (CH)
	Plane crash at Beamsley of a Canadian crewed Lancaster which hit the side of the hill in thick fog on a training exercise from RAF Leeming. Four dead and four survivors (CH) *(see*

	Chapter 4).
16 November	A year of good work for NFU (Addingham and Ilkley branch) (IG)
	Miss Eileen Blakeney Flynn, only daughter of Addingham Rector, married Major Peter McKenzie Smith MC, Queens Own Yorkshire Dragoons, eldest son of late Colonel I K Smith SO, CBE. Bridegroom served in Palestine and Syria with 8th Army in the Middle East and finally in Italy, where awarded MC for gallantry in the field. Serving now in Airborne Forces and attached to Parachute Regiment. Bride served with ATS since 1939 and was recently released from service with rank of Junior Commodore (CH)
	More complaints to Parish Council about the positioning of bus stops, and poor street lighting, in village (CH)

1946

4 January	Thomas Dean, head of office staff and cashier with Lister & Co, Low Mill, dies aged 58 (IG)
11 January	Strong criticism that Memorial Close was the most suitable site for housing in Addingham – raised at Parish Council meeting on 7 January. *'Skipton Rural Council should not view sites without having Parish Council or District Council members from village present'* (IG)
	Corporal T Glenn, 28 Main Street, is in charge of all transport arrangements at RE HQ Company, 53rd Welsh Infantry Division, at present constructing a Bailey bridge across The Rhine at Wesel. All his vehicles have seen war service and yet all well maintained and breakdowns are rare (IG)
	Knitting Circle: last meeting 8 January 1946. Over 3,000 garments knitted for Addingham service men/women. Over 500 articles sent to occupied countries, others sent to Russia, and considerable amounts of second-hand clothing for evacuees. Spent £1,000 in sending Christmas gifts – money derived from house collections, whist drives and dances and gifts from public (CH)
12 January	Special meeting of Parish Council to discuss housing sites in Addingham (CH)
25 January	Addingham woman killed by belladonna poisoning, self-

News in Wartime

	inflicted, in a cup of tea. Open verdict. She had a sad personal life, some men friends (IG) Freehold of house at 6 Parkinson Fold sold for £305 (IG) Danger at Crown corner in Addingham (IG) Anger at powers of delivering the mail being taken away from the village – change is costing more money (IG) Talent Competition, final event of Welcome Home and Remembrance Fund. 20 entries in 2 groups: over and under 14 years old (CH)
13 February	Addingham Nursing Association: Two successful Whist Drives held. (IG)
15 February	Transport and lighting problems still worrying Parish Council – inadequate street lights in part, last buses, numbers of buses and location of bus stops (CH)
22 February	Over £1,320 raised by Addingham 'Welcome Home and Remembrance Fund'. £5 would be available for each man and woman in services during War (IG)
1 March	Rider taking part in Bradford & District Motor Club, Jack Ellis of Leeds, aged 23, collapsed and died while talking to Phyllis Robinson and others on Cocking Lane, Addingham Moorside. He had a long-standing heart problem (IG)
8 March	39% poll in WRCC election in Addingham. J Wood (Conservatives) 2,746, A Snowden (Labour) 1,094 – Majority 1,652 (IG)
15 March	Parish Council: £250 precept for lighting streets (IG) Villagers anxious for public meeting to deal with money collected for war memorials (IG) 16 cases of dried fruit to Skipton Rural Council from South Africa: *'how many old age pensioners and people living alone would like the fruit?'* (IG)
29 March	Precept £350 at the annual meeting. Addingham ratepayers on Monday agreed that letting of land should be advertised so that all ratepayers would be aware of the fact (CH)
12 April	Annie Bell, Fell Edge Farm, Moorside, was bus conductress on a service up South Hawksworth Street which ran over John Martin Warren of South Hawksworth Street. He had crossed to the north side and then run back to the south side. He died of his injuries (IG)
18 April	Jack Bradley, an Addingham native living in London SW7, broadcast on BBC Light Programme on Easter Tuesday –

	'They're Out', a variety feature composed of ex-Servicemen artists. Son of William Bradley, an Addingham textile engineer, he gave impressions, for 7 minutes, of some famous film stars. Educated at Bradford Grammar School. Recently returned from Middle East Forces after serving in Cairo Forces Broadcasting Station (IG)
19 April	Form of War Memorial for the village: a public meeting, wanted a village hall providing and Knitting Circle had already provided £50 for this purpose. Committee will prepare a scheme, find a site, and get out plans for future public meeting (CH)
3 May	Addingham Nursing Association: District Nurse, in 1945, made 2900 visits to 115 patients. 22 student nurses in area from West Riding to learn rural district nursing (IG)
17 May	Mt Hermon Church anniversary (CH)
5 July	Football Club revival, they last played in 1939 (CH)
19 July	Addingham Fete and Gala organised by committee of Post-War Memorial Fund, in conjunction with Children's Sports Day (CH)
26 July	Jack Bradley to broadcast again. He is to compére 'Frivolities Show' from the Playhouse, Weston-super-Mare (IG)
16 August	Repair to fencing on Low Mill Lane where recent drowning tragedy occurred (CH)
23 August	Ted Hudson, Cockshott Place, who served in both the Boer War and the First World War, dies aged 66 (IG)
20 September	Rev Blakeney Flynn dies suddenly from a seizure on 5 September 1946. For 16 years Rector of Addingham (IG)
27 September	Gifts from Australia: Addingham receives 40 tins of meat, 10 tins of fruit and 20 packets of toffee (CH)
11 October	Lister Ellis, aged 92, still walks to Ilkley from his Addingham home in less than an hour (IG)
18 October	Parish Council writing to MP re. public conveniences in Addingham and the need for more new houses. *'16 homes should have been up by now, but land not even bought yet'*. Parliamentary seats' re-distribution: recommendations are cancelled (CH)
15 November	3 lamp standards being removed from Bark Lane and Springfield Mount to be re-erected in areas of village badly in need of light. This is due to the difficulty of obtaining new

	street lamp standards (CH)
	Poppy Day collection in village realises £40 (CH)
18 November	Complaints still on-going regarding Addingham roads and houses (IG)
27 December	John William Smith dies, aged 66. He was a veteran of Kitchener's Army (IG)

Chapter 3
The Addingham men who fell during WW2

Here follows details of the men from Addingham who lost their lives in the war. 15 of these are listed on the Addingham War Memorial but one is not, as indicated in the details.

BRACE, Eustace Frank Feilden, 2nd Lt.

Born 16th May 1920 in the Paddington District of London. Residence: Lincolnshire.

Eustace was the son of Colonel Henry Fergusson DSO MC (1888-1948) and Beatrice Ida Feilden (1892-1973). His parents divorced in 1936 and his father remarried (1937) to Susan Agnes Rhodes Tilney of Grantham, Lincolnshire.

His mother remarried (1936) to Major James Haggas and divorced in 1948. Lived at High House, Moorside Lane.

Eustace was educated at Eton and Sandhurst and passed out second on the list for commissions.
He was 'Gazetted' in July 1939 to the 15/19 King's Royal Hussar's, which was the regiment that his father commanded from 1930 to 1934.

On 10th May 1940, he was posted to C Squadron of the Hussars and sent to patrol the Pecq Bridge, over the river Escaut in Belgium, but did not report any enemy activity over the next day or so. However, on the 18th May, he was sent out to patrol and reconnoitre the main road in the village of Wolvertham, near to the cities of Ghent and Antwerp, but, soon after he set out, wireless communication with his unit was lost. It later transpired that his troop had run into some German tanks near Wolvertham and had been badly shot up. Eustace, who was troop leader, was killed instantly – the first officer-casualty of the war in NW Europe and the fourth man to be killed in the 15/19 Hussars.

Corporal Payne (later mentioned in dispatches), although badly wounded, made his way back on foot to British Lines and related what had happened.

As well as in Addingham, Eustace is commemorated at St. Werburgh's Church and War Memorial at Hanbury in Staffordshire and at St Sebastian Church in Great Gonerby near Grantham, Lincolnshire.

Eustace Frank Feilden Brace Second LT, aged 20 years, died 18th May 1940. Royal Armoured Corps. He is buried, along with 237 identified British soldiers and 32 unidentified, in ADEGEM (Canadian) Commonwealth Military Cemetery Belgium.

834 Canadian soldiers are buried there and 11 unidentified. Also some from New Zealand, France, and Poland. The cemetery is located midway between Brugge and Gent.

DICKSON, George

According to local residents, it is thought that the above name on the Addingham War Memorial refers to a George Dickson who lived at Farfield Cottages, Addingham. He was employed as a gardener/chauffeur at Farfield Hall. His father had also worked for Mr George Douglas as a domestic chauffeur at Farfield Hall.

At the moment, no service records are available (classified) from the MOD. for those wounded, or with ill health, and who died at home. Also, some of the WW2 records were destroyed during the war. So far, no records have been found with reference to a George Dickson from Addingham, who died during the war.

George Dickson, from the above address, is buried in St Peters Churchyard. Born 1912 and died June 29th, 1945, aged 33 years, his cause of death was pulmonary tuberculosis. His wife, Kathleen Dickson (1903 – 1987), is also buried there.

In the Ilkley Gazette dated 4th July 1941, it was stated *'George Dickson was added to the list of Addingham men now in the forces (now totals 148)'*. Also, from the

Gazette archives, George Dickson is mentioned several times by acknowledgements from the Women's Knitting Circle for gifts received and he was still donating right up to the time of his death, when they acknowledged a gift received from him on the 29th June 1945 – the actual date of his death. Also, on the 13th July 1945, regrets were expressed at the death of *'a good supporter – George Dickson'*. (See Chapter 3)

There does not appear to be any descendant from the marriage and any siblings and nieces/nephews have either died or moved.

It may be that George Dickson was only in the forces for a short time and discharged on medical grounds (TB).

If anyone can give any information about him and his time in the forces please contact one of the authors. Thank You.

DRAKE, James

A native of Addingham, he later moved to 6, Burley Thwaites Avenue, Ilkley. James was employed as a gardener by Mr Stanley Waddilove, of Heathcote, King's Road, Ilkley, before he joined the Royal Marines in November 1940. He was reported missing when the cruiser HMS Charybidis was sunk during an action against enemy light naval forces in the English Channel in October 1943. His wife was notified, then, that he was missing, but it was not until January 1945 that she received official notification of his death, which stated *'It is with deep regret that I have to inform you that, according to a German broadcast, the body of your husband, Musician James Drake, was washed ashore on the Isle of Jersey and was buried in the Mont A L'Abbe Cemetery. It has therefore become necessary to presume his death occurred in October 1943. Please allow me to express, on behalf of the Officers and men of the Royal Navy and the Royal Marines, the high traditions which your husband helped to maintain, and sincere sympathy with you in your sad loss.'*

The light cruiser HMS Charybdis had left Plymouth on 22nd October 1943 and was torpedoed by German torpedo escorts to German blockage runner, the Munsterland. It was hit on the port side twice and sank within half an hour, with the loss of 400 men, but four officers and 103 ratings survived. The German force escaped unharmed. Munsterland was eventually forced ashore and destroyed on 21st January 1944 by fire from British Coastal Artillery.

Soon after the sinking of the Charybidis, the bodies of 21 Royal Navy and

Royal Marine men were washed up in Guernsey and the German Occupation Authorities buried them with full military honours. The bodies of 38 other men are buried on Jersey, at St. Helier, and a great many more are buried in France.

The wrecks of the Charybidis and Limbourne have been located. Charybidis was found in 1993 lying in 83 metres of water.

James Drake died 23rd October 1943 aged 32 years.
Memorial/Cemetery: St Helier War Cemetery, Howard-Davis Park, Jersey, Grave 25.

EGAN, Laurence Michael

Known as Laurie, he lived near the Mount Hermon Chapel, in a house which was later demolished to allow Bolton Road to be widened. They were Irish and he had a sister Mary. His uncle, Laurie McRink, was killed in W.W.1. Laurie was previously employed by Messrs James Adams Ltd of Addingham and he was a popular member of the Athletic Club.

He joined up in May 1941 and was a Gunner in the Royal Artillery. He was sent overseas in December 1941but was posted missing whilst serving with the Royal Artillery Indian Command. It was later confirmed that he had been killed instantly on the 17th March 1944, aged 22.

Laurence Egan, Gunner, Service No. 1800 531, Died 17th March 1944, Grave: Memorial Face 2, Rangoon Memorial (CWGC)

> **The Rangoon Memorial** is in the centre of the Taukkyan war cemetery which is a cemetery for allied soldiers from the British Commonwealth who died in battle in Burma during the Second World War. The cemetery is in the village of Taukkyan about 25 kilometres north of Yangon. The cemetery contains the graves of 6,374 soldiers who died in the Second World War and 52 soldiers who died in Burma during the First World War.
>
> The Rangoon Memorial has the names of over 27,000 Commonwealth soldiers who died in Burma during the Second World War who have no known grave. There are 867 graves that contain the remains of unidentified soldiers. It is one of the most visited and highly rated war sites of all Asia. (CWGC)

FOSTER, George William

Born 13th September 1904 at Chapel Lane (Street) and named George William but known as 'Billie' or 'Willie', he was the only son of Mr & Mrs Stephen Foster. He later lived at 4, Daisy Hill, and had a sister called Fanny.

Addingham men who fell

Prior to joining the forces he was employed as a chauffeur-gardener for Mr Holmes, of Oakhouse, Ilkley, who later moved to Goodwood, Ilkley, for over ten years.

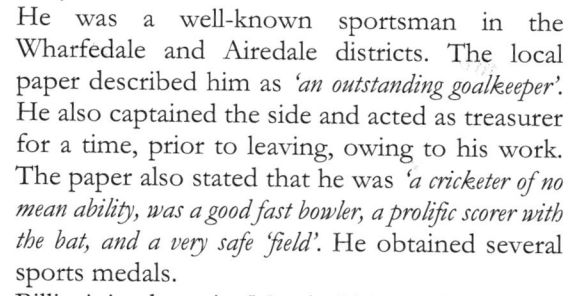

He was a well-known sportsman in the Wharfedale and Airedale districts. The local paper described him as *'an outstanding goalkeeper'*. He also captained the side and acted as treasurer for a time, prior to leaving, owing to his work. The paper also stated that he was *'a cricketer of no mean ability, was a good fast bowler, a prolific scorer with the bat, and a very safe 'field'*. He obtained several sports medals.

Billie joined up in March 1941 (volunteered), becoming a Trooper of the 3rd County of London Yeomanry, in the Armoured Corps. By this time he was married with two young children and lived at Crossbanks. During the war, he went overseas, to the Middle East, and was involved at the start of the first Battle of El Alamein (1st July - 27th July 1942.) This was a battle of the Western Desert Campaign, fought in Egypt, between axis forces (Germany & Italy) of the Panzer Army Forces (known, also, as the Afrika Korps), commanded by Field Marshall Rommel, (nicknamed 'The Desert Fox'), and allied forces of Britain, India, Australia, South Africa, and New Zealand, of the 8th Army, commanded by General Sir Claude Auchinleck and, later, by Field Marshall Montgomery. The British prevented a second advance by the axis forces into Egypt but were stopped by the German and Italian forces who had 'dug in' to allow exhausted troops to regroup.

The second Battle of El Alamein (October 23rd - November 5th, 1942), between the British 8th Army, led by Montgomery, and the Afrika Korps, near the town of Alamein, resulted in a decisive allied victory, which turned the tide of the war in Africa. With this victory, the British Army had prevented the Axis forces from occupying Egypt and capturing the Suez Canal, which was the access gate to the Middle Eastern oil fields.

Billie died from wounds at the beginning of the 1st Battle of El Alamein in the 14th Casualty Clearance Station. His wife Dora received official notification and later had a letter from a comrade/friend: *'I had hoped that he would recover from his wounds but that was not to be. It is a terrible tragedy for you, but I am sure that he has not given his life for his country in vain.'* His children were Frank, not quite six years old, and Kathleen, almost 4 years old when their father died. Kathleen Lister (née Foster) still lives in the village. When their father went to war she was in Leeds Hospital and her father called to see her before he went away but was not allowed into the ward and only saw her from a distance. (In those days, visiting was very restricted and only allowed on certain days and during certain times.)

However, a Mrs Briggs (of Addingham), who her mother had worked for, met someone who knew the Captain of the section and was able to send an air mail letter to inform her father that *Kathleen is doing splendidly, is very happy, and the doctors very pleased with her'.* The family received a Christmas card in 1941, signed 'Billie', from Egypt. A postcard, with the photo of his children on, was with his belongings:

Billie is on the left   *Billie, with Kathleen & Frank on the right*

At St Peters Church, at Evensong, a special service was given by the Rector Blakeney Flynn for G W Foster, the first casualty from the parish, and all those reported missing in the war. The Rector stressed the importance of manly keenness, ready sacrifice, and Christian immortality.

G. W. 'Billie' Foster, Trooper, Royal Armoured Corps 3rd County of London Yeomanry died on the 8th July 1942 aged 37 years. He is buried in the El Alamein War Cemetery, Ref X11 J16.

HILLMAN, Neville Walton

The only son of Mr & Mrs Frederick Hillman and a grandson of the Rev S D Hillman who was, for many years, Minister of the Ilkley Congregational Church. His mother was the daughter of Mr & Mrs Walton, Addingham.

Neville attended the Dental School at Leeds University and carried out his profession as a dental surgeon in his residence at Laurel Bank, Addingham. He joined the R.A.F and was granted a commission as a Flying Officer for the duration of hostilities, on the 26th November 1940. Military No. 88374. (London Gazette 20th Dec.1940). Nearly a year later the same paper reported that Flying Officer Hillman had relinquished his Commission, on account of ill health, on 5th August 1941, and he died, at home, on the 17th January 1945, aged 44 years, with his sister Genevieve present at his death. He was interred at St Peters Church on the 20th January 1945 and the obituary in the local paper mentioned that Neville Walton Hillman died after a lingering illness (his death certificate stated that he died from Hodgkins Disease).

After his death, his sister moved to the seaside and ran a guest house for a few years but she died on 21st October 1949, aged 51 years, and is interred next to her brother at St Peters Church.

MELVILLE, John Simpson

The Ilkley Gazette, 16th Oct 1942, reported that 'Mrs Melville, of 29, Low Mill Lane, Addingham, has received news that her husband, Gunner John S Melville, has been killed in action while serving in the Middle East.

He left this country in April of this year. He has one son. Before joining up two years ago Gunner Melville was for nine years a bus conductor with the West Yorkshire Company at Ilkley'.

John S Melville died 2nd Oct.1942 aged 34 years. Royal Artillery. EL Alamein War Cemetery. Grave ref XX111.E.13

El Alamein Cemetery, Egypt, contains the graves of men who died at all stages of the Western Desert Campaign, brought in from a wide area, but especially those who died in the Battle of El Alamein at the end of October 1942 and in the period immediately before that.
The cemetery now contains 7,240 Commonwealth burials of the Second World War, of which 815 are unidentified. There are also 102 war graves of other nationalities.
The Alamein Memorial is a Commonwealth War Graves Commission war memorial which commemorates 11,866 commonwealth forces members who died during world war two with no known grave.

MILBURN, Dennis Charles

Dennis joined up in May 1940 as a Guardsman in the Coldstream Guards. He was the elder son of Mr & Mrs George Milburn of Church Street and, before joining up, he was employed at the Hamilton Quarry, Bolton Abbey. Both Dennis, his only brother, Eddie, and their father were in the church choir at St Peters Church. Guardsman Eddie Milburn, was transferred to the Coldstream Guards after entering the RAF from the Ilkley Squadron of the ATC.

Dennis went overseas on D-Day plus 10, but he came back to England in July suffering from a poisoned leg. He returned to active service at the end of August and was in action on the Western Front when he was killed instantly while moving forward, with his section, through Berge, a small town east of Lingen, not far from the Dutch border, during a week in which the 'Ruhr pocket' was finally eliminated and a truce had been called at the nearby town of Celle to allow the British to take over the Belsen concentration camp.

> The campaign of the Western Desert was fought between the Commonwealth forces (with later, the addition of two brigades of Free French and one each of Polish and Greek troops) all based in Egypt and the axis forces (German & Italian) based in Libya. The battlefield across which the fighting surged back and forth between 1940 and 1942, was the 1,000 kilometres of desert between Alexandria in Egypt and Benghazi in Libya. It was a campaign of manoeuvre and movement, the objectives being the control of the Mediterranean, the link with the east through the Suez Canal, the Middle East oil supplies and the supply route to Russia through Persia.

One of his Officers paid tribute to Dennis in a letter to his parents. In expressing the sympathy of all the company he stated *'It was the Platoon's job, on that afternoon, to move up a street, and your son was Acting Second-in-Command, and Bren-Gunner, of No 2 Section. With his corporal and a third man, your son came into an open space of ground round the corner of a house and, I am sorry to say, they came under fire from a sniper on the opposite side of the road. Dennis was shot near the heart, and his Section Commander was hit as he was turning to go back. I came up a short time after, but both were dead, and must, therefore, have died instantly. He was a grand chap, your son, and very much liked by the whole Company. He was always cheerful and ready with a smile. If there was a job to be done he was always there. It was all the sadder as he was determined to see this job through to the end."* (report from the Ilkley Gazette)

Dennis Charles Milburn died 18th April 1945 aged 24. Coldstream Guards. Grave/Memorial: Rheinberg War Cemetery, Grave ref. 12.A.21.

> The site of the Rheinberg War Cemetery was chosen by the Army Graves Service for the assembly of Commonwealth Graves recovered from numerous War Cemeteries in the area. There are now 3,326 Commonwealth servicemen of the Second World War buried or commemorated at Rhineberg War Cemetery. 156 of the burials are unidentified. The town of Rheinberg lies in the west of Germany, north of Duisburg. (CWGC)

NEWTON, Stephen

Stephen volunteered for the RAF in February 1941 and was called up in September of the same year. Prior to joining up, he was employed at Brears' Sawmills and was an active and popular member of the Athletic Club.

Addingham men who fell

He was the only son of Mr & Mrs Charles Newton of Moor Lane and his father was well known in the public life of the village and a member of the Parish Council. Prior to joining the local Special Constables, he was one of the first to join the Air Raid Wardens in the village. During WW1 he was a Sergeant in the West Yorkshire Regiment, being invalided out after three years' service. He was employed for 23 years at the Post Office in Bradford.

Stephen was sent out to Canada for training and, apart from his duties as a Wireless Operator and Air Gunner, he was doing well with his studies. In a letter to his parents, received, ironically, on 29 May 1944 (Whit Monday), he referred to sitting an exam and looking forward to gaining a Commission. Stephen's parents received official information, by cable, shortly afterward, that Stephen had been killed in a flying accident on 24th May 1944.

The following report is about the No.5 Bombing and Gunnery School, Defoe, Saskatchewan, where Stephen was training, and gives details of the investigation after the fatal accident.

The largest training schools in Saskatchewan were the two Bombing & Gunnery schools dedicated to training bomb aimers and aerial gunners. One was at Defoe and the other at Mossbank. There were also nine service flying schools in Saskatchewan.

May 24th 1944 was a particularly dark day for the Number 5 BGS, with the loss of five airmen.

Pilot Officer Frederick Butcher of the RCAF was assigned to Bolingbroke 9881 for a routine camera gun exercise. Pilot Officer Butcher was very experienced, having completed a tour of operations in Europe during which he accumulated 297 hours of flying time in Bristol Blenheims, the British version of the Bolingbroke. He had also completed a refresher training course before joining No.5 BGS for six months prior to the date of this accident, and had accumulated another 172 hours in them. He was known by superior officers to be a steady, safe, experienced and competent pilot.

The crew of Bolingbroke 9881 completed their camera-gun exercise at approximately 9 am. Butcher was seen flying straight and level as he headed back toward No.5 BGS. However, a number of area farmers reported seeing Bolingbroke 9881 climbing and diving, as well as banking steeply to the left and to the right. Then they witnessed the aircraft's right wing suddenly dip and the plane fell into a spin, from an altitude of about four-to-five thousand feet. During the spin the engines sputtered and then quit. A couple of hundred feet above the ground the aircraft ceased spinning and dove straight into the ground at high speed. All aboard were killed on impact. The crash occurred 6 miles south-west of No.5 BGS.

After hearing what the witnesses had to say, the accident investigators concluded that the pilot had been engaging in prohibited aerobatics. Both the

Officer Commanding Armament Training and the Officer Commanding Gunnery Flight testified to the investigation that Butcher was a safe and reliable pilot with a good deal of experience on the type of aircraft he was flying that day. The Investigation Officer stated *'there can be no doubt that a pilot of the ability of (Butcher) would not attempt to spin a Bollingbroke from such a low altitude.'*

Still, mechanical failure was ruled out as the cause, after inspection of the wreckage. The engines had quit because they had been switched off – Butler had turned them off in order to prevent a fire when the aircraft struck the ground and so increase the chances of a least some on board surviving. No fire had occurred as a result of the crash.

The Accident Investigation branch concluded that the spin had been inadvertent, its exact cause could not be determined. However, the examination of the wreckage did show that the pilot's harness had not been fastened, which was contrary to the Station's standing orders. Because the pilot was not strapped in, he would have been thrown out of his seat by the force of the spin and therefore would have been unable to regain control of the aircraft. Even experienced veterans made fatal mistakes.

Those who died were:
Pilot Office Frederick Lloyd Butcher, aged 24, from Solsgirth, Manitoba.
Warrant Officer William David Mitchell, aged 23, from Prince Albert, Saskatchewan.
L.A.C Stephen Newton, aged 21, from Yorkshire, England.
L.A.C Howard John Lewis, aged 26, from Moorefield, Ontario.
L.A.C Stanley Edward Steeton, aged 18, from Colonsay, Saskatchewan.

(The above taken from 'Number 5 Bombing and Gunnery School, Defoe, Saskatchewan', by Stephen Carthy)

Stephen would have been out in Canada for just two years on June 1st and was there under the auspices of the Commonwealth Air Training Plan. This was a massive joint military aircrew training programme, created by the UK, Canada, Australia and New Zealand. Nearly half the pilots, navigators, bomb aimers, air gunners, wireless operators and flight engineers of the four air forces were trained under the programme.

Canada accepted the costs of the plan but, in return, insisted that Britain pronounced that air training would be Canada's primary war effort. Testimony to the high esteem in which Stephen was held was the large number of letters that were received by his parents, expressing sympathy. (as reported in the local paper.)

Stephen Newton, Leading Aircraftman, Royal Air Force Volunteer Reserve. Died 24th May 1944, aged 22 years.
Buried at Humboldt Municipal Cemetery, Saskatchewan, Grave ref: Soldiers Plot, Row 2, Grave 2

Addingham men who fell

ODDY, Geoffrey Willink

The youngest son of Mr & Mrs Oddy of Farfield Cottages, Bolton Road, his second name, 'Willink', was after a Cannon Willink, a friend of the family. He was educated at Ilkley Grammar School and, prior to joining the Navy, was employed as a transport clerk by Messrs Toulsans of Otley. A Leading Motor Mechanic, he served on a landing craft and had seen a good deal of invasion service He had been in the Service since 1941, and had just celebrated his 21st birthday, when he was killed by enemy action in August 1944.

His sister Elizabeth said that he was reported missing after the landing craft that he served on was hit by a mine 'offshore'. Although the family made many enquiries, over the years, to the Admiralty, his body was never recovered. The family received his war medals, and his name is on the War Memorial at Chatham.

His sister also remembers Geoffrey coming home for a short leave just a fortnight before his death: *'he had walked from Skipton Railway Station to his home at Farfield and walked back again in the dark to catch the train. Although he didn't have much time at home, he had placed the medals that he had won for sporting events on display in his bedroom'.*

Mr & Mrs Oddy's other two sons were also in the Forces: Capt. G H Oddy served with the Royal Artillery and Flight Sergeant E D Oddy with the Royal Air Force.

Note: On 25th August 1944 there was a series of actions involving motor torpedo boats in the English Channel, off the French coast, which involved a supply mission after the recapture of the port of Le Havre. There were also attacks off Fecamp and Cap d'Antifer, where several craft were lost.

Geoffrey Willink Oddy died 25th August 1944 aged 21years. His Memorial ref. Panel 84 Chatham Naval Memorial.

PERKINS, Thomas

Known as 'Tommy', he lived in Druggist Lane and was employed on the Ilkley Golf Links before the war, He was well known in Wharfedale football circles and led the Addingham Minors to win the shield in their first Season. (Ilkley Gazette, 1943)

Addingham in World War Two

Tommy served in a Territorial Army Unit as a Lance Bombardier and was in France at the time of the evacuation of Dunkirk, later going on to North Africa. His brother Jack served with the Royal Artillery. Tommy was killed in action and a letter from the Rev. F. Hunter, the Chaplain attached to the unit, was sent to his parents *(shown with Tommy in the photo)*, in which he expressed sympathy:-
'I expect you will have received the sad news by the time this letter arrives, that your son was killed in action. I felt I must write to you and tell you of our very great sympathy for you in your loss, for I can understand how you are feeling. He was killed when an enemy shell fell on his gun troop position, and he was killed at once. He has been buried close to the scene of action, and we were able to have some prayers'. He added that L/Bdr Perkins *'was greatly liked and his Officers spoke most highly of him'*.

A year after his death, a former comrade, Bdr. Earl, had seen in the local paper (IG) a Memoriam Notice concerning Bdr. Perkins and he sent a letter to the family saying, *'we all thought a lot of Tom and it came as a great blow to us when he was killed.'* He also enclosed verses written by one of his colleagues, F. Dunn, dedicated to the men who fell in the battle of Sedjanane, North Africa on March 3rd 1943. The verses tell of the outward voyage, the fighting, and the burial of the dead. The original handwritten poem (below) has been kept

Addingham men who fell

in the family and is now in the possession of Tommy's niece, Mrs Pauline Wild (née Perkins), who kindly forwarded this copy of the original. Here is a transcription:-

LEST WE FORGET

'My comrades and I know well the day
We packed our kits and sailed away
We sailed by day and we sailed by night
And for ten solid days no land in sight.
Then came one Sunday morning bright
We saw Algiers 'twas a wonderful sight
Two weeks went past then came the day
We limbered our guns and went on our way
We went on and on till our journey was done
And we came face to face with our enemy, the Hun.
For three long weeks, we ne'er fired a shot
Till one fine morn', the Hun made it hot
We left our positions we thought all was well.
When all around us our comrades fell
As we dug their graves side by side
We turned away our tears to hide,
We dug them wide we dug them deep
And placed shell cases around their feet
Then placed a cross above their head
Lest we forget the fallen dead.
But now it's all over the battle is won
We must not forget them not even one
Their blood was shed for a country so rare
And now we must leave them lying out there
But the day will come when we can tell
Of how in battle our comrades fell
Lest We Forget.'

F.Dunn

Thomas Perkin's niece Pauline never knew her Uncle Tommy as she was born the year that he died but she said *'we are all very proud of him, he was a brave young man'*. The original poem will be passed on to the next generation of the Perkins family.

Mr Dunn, who wrote the poem, was also an Addingham man and it referred to the battles of Sedjenane from February-March and April-May 1943 (see box below).

Thomas Perkins died 3rd March 1943 aged 23 years. Grave Ref. 2 A I Tabarka Ras Rajel War Cemetery, Tunisia. *(Tabarka is a coastal town on the Tunisian/Algerian border. The War Cemetery is some 12 kilometres east of the town.)*

Sedjenane is a town in Northern Tunisia, on the railway line to Mateur and the Port of Bizerta. The town became of strategic importance during the Allied invasion of North Africa in WW2. Following the initial landings of Operation Torch, the Allied run for Tunis was halted by German Paratroopers. The German advance held by a series of counter-attacks by the British and Italians. **Severe casualties between both sides on 2nd and 3rd March; the date when Tommy Perkins was killed.** The town finally fell to the Germans and Italians on 4th March. In the Second Battle of Sedjenane (April–May1943) the town was retaken by the Allies on 1st April. The several Allied counter-attacks through March 1943 to first stem the German advance and then retake Sedjenane represented the first time that British and German Parachute Troops had fought each other. The use of the term 'Red Devil' to describe a British Paratrooper reputedly has its origins in these engagements, fought by men of the 1st Parachute Brigade. The American Forces took over positions in the Sedjenane area from 12th April, through to the conclusion of the North African Campaign in May 1943.

STAPLETON, Jack

Jack and George Stapleton were twin brothers who served together during the war.

During their service overseas, the Stapleton brothers had met only one local man – Willie Thompson, of Ilkley, who formerly lived at Moor Lane and who played for the Addingham and Ilkley British Legion football teams. They met in San Marino.

Addingham men who fell

Two Little Boys
by Jack Stapleton jnr.

George (left) & Jack

The following article has been written by Jack Stapleton, the son of George Stapleton, who was the twin brother of Jack, from recollections of his father and written accounts from archives of the battalion in which they served.

The writer was also born in Addingham and also served in the army, for 24 years, in the Corps of Royal Electrical and Mechanical Engineers, as a Recovery Mechanic, from 1966 to 1990, and held the rank of Warrant Officer. His grandfather Matthew, also born in Addingham, served as a sergeant in the Durham Light Infantry in the First World War from 1914 to 1918. He was wounded twice in action.

'Jack Stapleton was born in Addingham, at Wesley Place, on the 23rd July 1919. In his teenage years he played football for Addingham, and was an active member of the local Gymnastics Club and the Wharfedale Cycling Club. He was an apprentice loomer & twister at Townhead Mill up to the time of being 'called up' into the army, aged 20, along with his twin brother George. He was then living at 'Westcliffe' on Moor Lane.

They were enlisted into the West Yorkshire Regiment on the 15th December 1939 and were then both transferred into the newly formed 8th Battalion of the Kings Own Royal Regiment (4th of Foot) on the 18th April 1940.

The Kings Own were part of the British Expeditionary Force (France) and was one of the regiments that had been instructed to defend the beaches at Dunkirk to allow the some 330,000 troops to evacuate the beaches and embark on to the 887 craft, which were all shapes and sizes, that had made their way to Dunkirk to evacuate the troops which had been pressed back by the might of the German army; they were among the last to come off the beaches at Dunkirk.

Once back in England they were deployed on anti-invasion duties on coastal defence in the south west of England, taking over a sector which included the towns of Exmouth, Budleigh-Salterton and Sidmouth; they also spent some time in the Isles of Scilly, and the many 'Pill Boxes' that are still to be seen today are evidence of their efforts to help defend Britain should Hitler's forces decide to invade.

They were then transferred up to Kelso for special training; on the 11th July 1941 they embarked from Glasgow on the cruiser HMS Manchester which was to be part of an un-divulged expeditionary force, then part of a convoy which included the aircraft carrier HMS Ark Royal, the cruiser HMS Arethusa, the battleships HMS Nelson & HMS Renown and 8 destroyers. The convoy sailed into darkness at 01:30 on July 21st 1941 and, when day broke, it revealed a great force of warships guarding the many merchant vessels, which were laden with all sorts of goods.

It was not until the ships had been at sea for a few days that all ranks were informed that their destination was Malta. HMS Manchester, carrying the majority of the 8th battalion, was torpedoed between Gibraltar and Malta.

An extract from a written account explains the scene: *'That quarter of an hour was a nightmare. Heavy Italian bombers flew high across the convoy at right angles and dropped a number of bombs on the merchant ships in the centre of the convoy, this was immediately followed by a torpedo-bomber attack coming from the port bow, flying very low at fifty to a hundred feet right between the lines of the ships.*

Columns of water went up as the bombs and torpedoes struck the surface: a destroyer was soon burning furiously and all the water around it: the noise of the guns was deafening, including light and heavy anti-aircraft armament and also the 'pompoms' (automatic antiaircraft cannon which produced puffs of smoke).

From the C.O's post on the lower bridge of HMS Manchester he could see the line of a torpedo on the surface of the water, rapidly approaching, it looked as though it must hit her amidships but the helm was put over and it actually struck aft on the port side. The torpedo had entered the cruiser aft of the armour and exploded, she seemed to stop dead and then lunge forward and there was an ominous list to port. The noise was terrific, lights went out, fuel oil pipes were cut and oil gushed and flooded in all directions. It was only after it had been stemmed a little that it was possible to begin rescue operations. There were some sixty bodies slumped in unconscious heaps, black and shiny with oil, that had been behind the locked waterproof doors which stopped the Manchester sinking; on her way, limping, back to Gibraltar three Italian planes attempted to molest HMS Manchester and all aboard felt she was a sitting target as the after guns could not be used for fear of breaking her back'.

Jack (left) and George

On the 25th, all that had been killed were buried at sea and the Manchester docked in Gibraltar on the 27th July 1941. Later, in dry dock, it was observed that the hole the torpedo made was large enough to drive a double decker bus through.

In broad daylight, on the 30th July 1941, the battalion boarded the French converted troopship HMT Pasteur, hoping to delude observers on the Spanish shore into thinking that the Kings Own was going back to England; nothing could have been further from the truth.

In the dead of night, at 01:00 on the 1st August 1941, the battalion left HMT Pasteur with great secrecy and boarded HMS Hermione, Arethusa and the minelayer Manxman, for it had been decided that the best way of getting the battalion through was to carry the whole of it in warships, all of which could steam at speed; the Manxman was especially fast, being capable of 40 knots. The party left together, zig-zagging to avoid submarines, and when dawn broke cloudy the hope was justified, that the ships would not be seen.

They landed on Malta on the 2nd August 1941, the HQ of the Kings Own was based at Luqa aerodrome. Initially, they were responsible for defending the island and the airfield. Jack became a dispatch rider on the island and experienced the full pounding during the great siege of Malta by the Germans. On almost every fine day, from the 1st January 1942 until well into May, there were usually three heavy raids, sometimes as many as five, and each raid had anything up to a hundred and fifty bombers.

Later, they were sent to North Africa and Palestine, where they were amalgamated with the 1st Battalion who had taken heavy losses on the Greek Dodecanese island of Leros; only 55 had survived out of the battalion. An agreement was reached where the 8th Battalion should assume the identity of the 1st Battalion, the reconstituted Battalion landed at Taranto in Italy on the 28th March 1944, left Taranto on the 19th April, and landed up on the front line on the 23rd April 1944.

The 1st Kings Own advanced east of the river Tiber, on the 30th June 1944 the battalion put in its first attack since its reconstitution, all objectives were taken and also a number of prisoners. As the battalion approached Umbertide, a market town twenty miles north of Perugia, resistance from the enemy stiffened. The battalion continued to be successful in a number of minor operations, amongst which was an attack on Pierantonio on the 3rd July, a village overlooked by a hill which was strongly defended. To the east of Umbertide, which the 1st battalion entered at the head of the division, the enemy made a stand in strength along a stream between Montone and Carpini.

Montone was the key to the position; standing upon a high hill with steep bare approaches which were strongly defended it dominated the whole Tiber valley and several attempts to capture it were repulsed with heavy loss, but the Kings Own, when called upon to attack it, planned to do so from the rear, and at 9.30 pm on the 6th July the battalion swung away on a twelve mile night march across difficult and little-reconnoitred country. The men were in single file, closed right up, they crossed five ravines with scarcely a track to indicate the easiest route, along great features, through woods and across fields, and then down a slope across the Pietralunga road, and up a steep and difficult incline. It seemed they would never reach the top.

So far, the column had moved in complete silence, not a word was spoken and the sound of marching was deadened by the soft ground, but suddenly a dog barked from a farm house and in the stillness of the night it seemed enough to warn every German for miles around; the wretched animal continued to bark furiously while the battalion filed past.

The strain was beginning to tell and as the men climbed up and up they gasped for breath, but at last, unseen and unopposed, they arrived below their first objective, Monte Cucco, the feature which dominated, from the rear, their second objective, the village of Montone. An 'O' Group was called, after which the Commanding Officer (CO) led the battalion to the very top of Monte Cucco from where Montone could be seen silhouetted in the moonlight.

Owing to the exhaustion of the troops it was decided to postpone the attack until 7am and an anxious quarter of an hour ensued while the gunners worked furiously to establish contact with the guns and postpone the opening bombardment.

Then followed hours of stiff house-to-house fighting, in which all the advantage was with the defenders. The place was a maze of streets and alleyways, most of them effectively covered by German machine guns, which made the task of clearing the town very difficult. Enemy heavy machine gun fire ensued, but the battalion eventually accomplished their aim and what the enemy believed to be an impregnable fortress was destroyed; the entire German company being captured or killed in the action.

There followed a month of slow, difficult advance against determined enemy rear guard action, in appalling weather. The first eight days of assaulting a series of knife-edged ridges were particularly unpleasant. Swollen rivers barred the way, which rose so rapidly that when the battalion had successfully crossed the Rubicon and was ordered to withdraw, it found that the river had risen so fast behind it that this could not be done. It remained isolated with no anti-tank support until the following day, roads and tracks were impassable.

The battalion served with distinction in the Tiber Valley, captured the village on Montone in July, and took part in the night attack which opened the road to Citta di Castello. In October the Battalion fought in the Adriatic sector, on the night of the 6th October the company he was in, led by his company commander, attacked and captured San Martino, followed by heavy fighting to secure and retain Pidura Ridge, west of Faenza, in December. Extracts of accounts tell that the weather was appalling between October and December 1944 and heavy losses were encountered. The intense fighting, and the handling of the situation, led to his company commander being awarded the Military Cross.

On the 16th December, in the Montone Valley, on Pedura Ridge, Jack, who was now the platoon's wireless operator, and had been sent to the front to report and observe enemy activity. He had been late in coming back and his brother George, and two other soldiers, were located in the loft of a shelled out building in a forward position, with the platoon PIAT *(a spring-powered British antitank weapon, mounted on a tripod and capable of firing a 2½-pound bomb up to 350 yards)*, to further observe and give covering fire if needed. There was a burst of machine gun fire and his brother George heard a cry. He went out to look and found that it was his twin brother Jack, who had been making his way back. It was raining heavily that night.

Jack died of wounds on his way to a Field Hospital, his twin brother George at his side. His company commander later wrote, in a letter to one of his soldiers, *'I remember being absolutely shattered when Jack was killed as I knew how badly it would affect George – I can still recall hearing him say "it's our kid" when he found him.'*

Their parents received a letter from the Padre of the Unit expressing sympathy and paying tribute to the character of both sons. They also received a letter from the Major of the Unit which said *'I would like to say that Jack was one of the best and most cheerful men in the Company. He was making an effort to get his wireless up to his Company H.Q. when he was shot. It is a great tragedy, as some of the men warned him not to go, but knowing the value of a wireless set and knowing his duty, he pushed on. It was a fine action, and I am only sorry that, as always, it is the best men and the most dutiful who are victims'.*

Jack is buried in the British Military Cemetery in Forli Italy, along with another 737 of the Second World War Commonwealth soldiers, not far from where he was killed; he was 25 years old.

Medals awarded to both Jack & George Stapleton were:

The 1939-45 Star, The Africa Star,

The Italy Star, The Defence Medal,

The 1939-45 War Medal,

The Dunkirk Veteran's Medal

Regimental numbers: Jack 4540873, George 4540874

Jack Stapleton, King's Own Royal Regiment, died 16th December 1944 aged 25 years. Grave ref. 1.B 21 Forli War Cemetery, Italy.

THOMPSON, William John Cunliffe

A casualty of WW2 and although not named on the war memorial there is a plaque inside St Peter's Church with the following inscription:

'In Memory of William John Cunliffe Thompson Sergeant Pilot RAF VR, only son of T C and E V Thompson. Killed in Action near Tobruk, Dec 11th 1941, age 24 years.'

His parents, Eleanor Violet Thompson, 1885–1965, and Thomas Coates Thompson, 1880-1968, are buried in St Peter's churchyard and the name of their son is also inscribed on their gravestone.

The Cunliffe, Lister, Coates, and Thompson families all have strong links with Addingham and the Church. (See *Addingham from Brigantes to Bypass* by Kate Mason) There are several plaques inside the church in their memory.

William John Cunliffe Thompson is buried in Knightsbridge War Cemetery (Grave ref.12.C.9) Acroma. Libya.

TURNPENNY, Ernest

Born 18th December 1913, the eldest son of William & Lucy Turnpenny. His father was a signalman and they lived at Station Cottages, Bolton Abbey, but then, when Ernest was about 5 years old, they moved to Station Cottage, 125 Main Street, Addingham.

Ernest worked as a clerical worker for the local railway and then for Bradford Dyers Association. He was living with his wife Ethel and young daughter

Beryl at 3 Hudson Yard when he 'joined up' in 1940. He was posted to the Royal Corps of Signals and did his training in North Wales before joining the No.6 Army Air Support Signal Section, which was formed in Kirkburton in September 1941 They embarked on the SS Empress of Canada at Gourock, for the Far East, via Cape Town, on the 3rd October 1941. The ship reached Singapore on 5th December, two days before Japan attacked Pearl Harbour. The Section then went by rail to Kuala Lumpur to join the 3rd Indian Corps of Signals and detachments were sent to various places in Malaya.

They were sent on to Segamat, which is a district located in the north of the state of Johor, in Malaysia, and, by 2nd February, to the Singapore area, where bombing and shelling very intense. By the 10th February their radio sets were destroyed and half of the Section was sent to assist the Military Police. Ernest was with the Section that took up defensive posts outside Singapore and suffered much shelling. The situation grew progressively worse, being shot at from all directions by the Japanese and their many supporters in the town. The water supply had been captured and ammunition was running short. Civilians and troops were dying by the thousand and, at last, the powers-that-be decided that the end had come. On the 15th February, Singapore surrendered to the Japanese. *'As they were marched through the town, death and destruction were everywhere; dead bodies lay by the roadside covered with flies, swollen by the heat and making a stench almost impossible to bear. Most of the houses flew the Rising Sun flag where, a few days earlier, had been the Union Jack. The locals had changed their allegiance and were now hostile'.*

Later, they were marched on to Changi, about 15 miles, with all possessions. Another of his comrades wrote *'The Royal Signals were quartered in the NAFFI building, rather a tight squeeze. The food was hardly adequate and medical stores and equipment were very deficient. From time to time, parties of men were sent out to Singapore to help with reconstruction; at least their departure eased the accommodation problem!*

After a few weeks, we were told that many men were to be 'sent north, to work on a big project', and glowing promises of improved conditions were made. The first party left for Siam on the 18th June, being sent to Non Pladuk, on the Bangkok to Singapore Railway, where the Burma to Siam Railway was to start. In June 1942 over 3,000 British soldiers left Changi by train and the next party, with Ernest, Ginger and me, left Singapore on 24th June, packed 24 in a truck half filled with sacks of rice. It was impossible for us all to sit down at the same time. This goods train was made up of windowless steel box waggons, with just a sliding door, we endured for five days and five nights. It was extremely hot during the day and very cold at night. Only once a day, for 30 minutes, the train stopped for our meal of cold, dirty, rice and to relieve ourselves. With the number of men suffering from diarrhoea, once a day was not enough and we had to ask two men to hold our hands whilst we hung out of the truck...

When we arrived at Ban Pong, on the edge of the town there was some evidence that the Japanese wanted to make reasonable provision, but the effort very soon faded. The first two huts were well constructed from wood, with boards for beds, but that soon tailed off. Then, when the rains came, the camp was flooded and quickly deteriorated into a morass. Everywhere was wet, hot, and steamy, and the camp was over-ankle-deep in thick black mud. The latrines were overflowing, mosquitoes abounded and, all in all, it was a squalid place. The men joked that this was the running water that the 'Japs' had promised us, among other mod cons! Over the coming months, a great many PoWs were force marched to the camps scattered along the railroad and the monsoons made movement, and work, very arduous. Ernest, with others, was then marched to Kanchanaburi (25miles) or to Chungkai.

The last letter that his wife received was at the end of January 1942 (before taken a PoW) and, in the letter, he mentioned that he had met Walter Millman, from Addingham, a few weeks earlier, in Malaya.

The local paper reported in **March 1942** (after the fall of Singapore) that they were both reported missing (see report on page 39). As no information was allowed out by the Japanese, his wife and family had to rely for news on letters from the War Office and it was not until after 16 months of not knowing whether her husband was alive or dead that, in **May 1943**, his wife received a letter from the War Office, and another from the Red Cross in **June** (below), giving her the 'good' news that he was a prisoner of war. At least that meant that he was alive when the report was sent but she was, very much later, to hear that she received it **several months after he had died.** It was not until the end of the war, on **30th June 1945,** that his wife received the news from the War Office (based on a report from a PoW who had recently returned to the UK after being recovered from the Japanese), that Ernest had died a PoW in **November 1942**. The letters that she received are shown opposite. For Official purposes, he was still recorded as a PoW until **November 1945,** when his death was officially confirmed by the War Office

This was a full three years after his actual death.

His Section Officer said later that he knew Ernest quite well. He wrote *'I attended his funeral with the other lads from the Section. He was a well-respected member of the Section. We lost 18 men, out of the Section of 50 men, in captivity, and they were all good lads. I believe he died from dysentery & malaria.*

Ernest Turnpenny, Royal Signals died 2nd November 1942 aged 28 years. Grave Ref 2G 40 Kanchanaburi Cemetery Thailand

Addingham men who fell

The letters received regarding Ernest Turnpenny which are referred to opposite:

WAR ORGANISATION OF THE BRITISH RED CROSS SOCIETY and ORDER OF ST. JOHN OF JERUSALEM

PW/FE/10/43

President: HER MAJESTY THE QUEEN.
Grand Prior: H.R.H. THE DUKE OF GLOUCESTER, K.G.

PRISONERS OF WAR DEPARTMENT

Chairman: MAJOR-GENERAL SIR RICHARD HOWARD-VYSE, K.C.M.G., D.S.O.
Deputy Chairman: J. M. EDDY, C.B.E.
Controller: S. G. KING

TELEPHONE No.: REGENT 0111 (5 LINES)
FAR EAST SECTION.

9, PARK PLACE,
ST. JAMES'S STREET,
LONDON, S.W.1

When replying please quote reference: FE. 18737.
23.6.43.

Mrs. E. Turnpenny,
3, Hudson Yd.,
Addingham.

Dear Mrs Turnpenny,

We have been officially advised that Sigln E. Turnpenny, Royal Signals, is a prisoner of war in Japanese hands. We are very glad that this news of his safety has at last been received.

Telephone: MAYFAIR 9400.
Your Ref.
W.O. Ref. 95752 Cas.P.W.

**THE WAR OFFICE,
CURZON STREET HOUSE,
CURZON STREET,
LONDON, W.1.**

30th June, 1945.

Madam,

I am directed to inform you with sincere regret that a report has been received from the prisoners of war who have recently arrived in the United Kingdom after being recovered from the Japanese in Luzon stating that a Signalman E. Turnpenny, Royal Signals (6 C.S.B.C. Draft), died whilst a prisoner of war in Thailand of malaria and dysentery in November, 1942.

The Department, unfortunately concludes that this statement must refer to your husband No.4543311 Signalman E. Turnpenny, Royal Signals (6th Army Air Supply Cont. Malaya).

While no confirmation of this distressing report has reached the Department from Japanese sources and no other details are available, it is considered that you should be informed of the news as received.

The Japanese authorities have been urged to send immediately any information of this nature relative to prisoners of war and should any confirmation of this distressing report or any further details be received you will, of course, be informed at once. In the meantime, for official purposes, he will remain recorded as a prisoner of war.

I am to convey the deep sympathy of the Department to you in the distress which this letter must inevitably cause.

I am, Madam,
Your obedient Servant,

Mrs. E. Turnpenny,
3, Hudson Yard,
Addingham.

Japanese Treatment of Prisoners of War

Japanese PoWs were refused the terms of the Geneva Convention as Japan had not ratified the PoW sections of the humanitarian code.

Prisoners were treated with contempt, and malnutrition, tropical diseases, cholera, and worm infestation, and a multiplicity of other ailments, took a high toll of PoW life. PoW doctors toiled to save life and limb, but, without any medical supplies and little food, large numbers began to die.

The Burma Railway, known as the 'Death Railway' because of the horrific conditions, and treatment of the prisoners, was a 258 mile railway line between Ban Pong, Thailand, and Thanbyuzayat, Burma. This railway completed a railway link between Bangkok in Thailand and Rangoon in Burma. Prewar surveys had shown that, because of the hostility of the terrain, such a project was impossible. Even if attempted it would take years to complete.

The Japanese Commanders were determined to establish an overland route which would avoid hazardous voyages around the Malayan Peninsular, so the Army Engineers were ordered to build the line, but to do it in 18 months. The only resource to turn to was human – it cost nothing and it was expandable. These PoWs, held in contempt, provided this resource in generous amounts.

It was started in June 1942 and completed in October 1943 with an estimated cost of 18,000 thousand lives, British, Australian, New Zealand, Dutch and American, not forgetting the estimated 90,000 – 100,000 Asian slave labourers who also perished. Some 200,000 were recruited from their occupied territories under the false pretences that they would have better pay and conditions. These unfortunate Asians lacked Army discipline and organisation and easily succumbed to the hardships inflicted upon them by the ruthless IJA.(Imperial Japanese Army). They had to endure dense jungle and terrible conditions; toiling with their bare hands and without machines. The conditions further up the line got even worse, men were very sick and dying by the hundred. When the railway was deemed to be behind schedule there was an almighty 'speedo' on. The Japanese were frantic, driving men well beyond their limits until they died or were so sick they could not stand up and were replaced by others. Beating was an everyday occurrence, dished out on any pretext. Day after day men would dig and hew in the feverish sun or teeming monsoon rain, driven on by guards wielding wire whips and bayonets. Perhaps the costliest part of the railway was the huge rock cutting section at Konyu, known as 'Hell Fire Pass'. Around 1,000 prisoners started work on it in April 1943 and by its completion, in August 1943, only 100 survived. Some beaten to death or dying from cholera, dysentery, starvation and/or pure exhaustion. It was virtually impossible to escape, one just could not survive long enough in the jungle to cover the distance to freedom. The few who tried were captured and either shot or beheaded.

The line was closed in 1947 but the section between Nong Pladuk and Nam Tok was re-opened 10 years later.

WALL, Hubert Prince

Hubert was born in 1915 and lived on Daisy Hill. His second name, Prince, was taken from his mother's maiden name. He had a brother, Norman, and a sister, who died, when twelve years old, from Diphtheria. Before joining the army Hubert was a mason and bricklayer engaged on Government work. After he married he went to live at 21, North Street, with his wife Florrie. They had two daughters.

He joined the Army in November 1942, as a Sapper in the Royal Engineers, and was in England until D-Day, when he took part in the invasion of France. He was killed in action by a sniper while building a bridge in Belgium. From further information, this happened near Zeebrugge during the week that the British and Canadians launched a heavy assault between the Leopold Canal and the South bank of the Scheldt, and two bridgeheads were established. This was only two weeks after the ill-fated Arnhem operation and the enemy was becoming increasingly difficult to dislodge in the northern Low Countries. The RAF breached the dyke on Walcheren Island, causing extensive flooding which damaged many of the enemies' defences. The Royal Engineers had a difficult time; repairing bridges led to tragedies as some bridges had been booby trapped by the retreating enemy, and a number of engineers fell to their deaths.

Hubert died at the age of 29, leaving his wife and their two daughters; Bessie aged 9 and Pat aged 2. He is buried in the Commonwealth plot of Blankenberge, Belgium, cemetery which contains 80 burials from WW2, fourteen of these unidentified. Blakenberge town cemetery is located on the coast of Belgium, four kilometres west of Zeebrugge.

Hubert Prince Wall, Royal Engineers, died 11th October 1944 aged 29 years. Grave Memorial: Row A, Grave 2, Blankenberge Cemetary, Belgium.

WOODFIELD, James Henry

Born in 1921, James was the only son of Mr & Mrs Woodfield. He had one sister. He was educated at Birdwell County Council School and he was employed at Lister's Low Mill prior to joining the Horse Guards. The family lived at 23, Low Mill.

James had been in the Army for over a year before the outbreak of War. He went abroad in October 1940 and served in the Middle East and throughout the Italian Campaign, coming home on leave in October 1944. At the beginning of 1945, he was sent out to the B.L.A *(the British Liberation Army – the official name given to British forces which fought on the Western Front in WW2 between the Normandy landings and VE Day. Almost all B.L.A units were assigned to 21st Army Group and were redesignated The British Army on the Rhine in August 1945).*

James was probably killed between Fallingbostel and Munster, in the same week that British and Canadian troops entered Bremen and the British Second Army reached Lubeck and Wismar. The day before his death British forces crossed the River Elbe near Lauenberg. His relatives probably received notification on or about VE day of him having been killed in action.

Fanatical fighting occurred in this area as the Germans, increasingly short of manpower, utilised more and more 'SS' and fanatical Hitler Youth. Even members of the German navy were drafted into the army. Many small villages were turned into strong points, particularly at road and rail junctions, and, generally, woods and hills became places of increasing resistance. Heavy losses were incurred on both sides in the final weeks of the war. Arnhem had been a warning of what, potentially, was to occur.

James Henry Woodfield Trooper (Royal Horse Guards) died 30th April 1945 aged 25 years. Grave/memorial ref. CO11. Grave 7.A 2-4, Becklingen War Cemetery, North Germany.

> The village of Beckilingen is approx 85 kms north of Hanover and the Becklingen War Cemetery is on a hillside overlooking Luneburg Heath. It was at Luneburg Heath, on 4th May 1945, that Field Marshall Montgomery accepted the German Surrender, from Admiral Doenitz.
> Burials were brought into this cemetery from isolated sites in the countryside, small German cemeteries, and PoW camp cemeteries, including the Fallingbostel cemetery.
> Most of those buried in the Beckilingen cemetery died during the last two months of the war. (CWGC)

Chapter 4
Two more wartime adventures

The men featured in the following stories both had Addingham connections, and survived the war, but had remarkable stories to tell:

Les Chamberlain

Les Chamberlain was brought up in Aylsham in Norfolk and started life as a land labourer catching rabbits and pigeons. He joined the Territorial Army in the thirties and transferred to the Second Battalion, Norfolk Regiment, in 1936.

On the outbreak of War, he was sent to France with other members of the British Expeditionary Force and spent months digging trenches and taking part in night convoy driving exercises and anti-parachutists training. The Germans invaded the Low Countries and France in May 1940 and, in spite of the BEF having numerical strength, the enemy had superiority in tanks and planes.

Hard fighting occurred, including the SS slaughtering 97 members of the 'C' Company of the Norfolk Regiment at Les Paradis; a terrible fate which Les only narrowly avoided. Soon, Les was captured and marched eastwards but, with two colleagues, managed to escape. His brother had hoped to escape with Les but he had been wounded and was to spend five years as a PoW. The three escapees were ambushed near the coast and a colleague was shot but Les and his remaining companion made contact with the Maquis *(French resistance fighters)* near Amiens. The Maquis helped them to reach Paris and eventually, under fire, cross the river border between Occupied France and Unoccupied France (governed by the Vichy Regime). On reaching Marseilles, they spent time in a Vichy-controlled fort and were then moved to another fort, nearer the Pyrenees, before entering Spain in April 1941 and returning home in June 1941.

Les was then sent to Denton, near Ilkley, to recover from his hair-raising time as an escaping PoW. Here he met his future wife at a dance at the Star Hotel in Ilkley and they were married in 1942. His daughter Brenda was born in May 1944. Les soon wanted to play his part in winning the war again and joined the newly formed Glider Regiment (Ox and Bucks). After training, he flew out on the night of 5/6 June 1944 (D-Day). They were 28 men in the glider, commanded by Major Howard, and, with two other gliders, landed almost next to Pegasus Bridge. He was the eleventh man out of the glider and helped to secure the bridge for the Allied forces. Soon, he was wounded and captured again by the Germans but was soon liberated by American troops from a military hospital in the city of Caen.

After the war, and recovering from shell shock, he worked for the Council in Ilkley and Addingham, including delivering the Royal Mail. Soon after his wife died in 1988, he met up with Major Howard and, later, Les decided to return to France and meet the surviving member of the Gondrée family, Arlette, and her British-born husband. The Gondrée family have owned the cafe by the Pegasus Bridge for over seventy years. Thereafter, until he died in 2001, Les annually visited the Café to talk to veterans and visitors about his experiences. He was happy, throughout his time in the Army, to be a Sergeant in the Norfolk Regiment and a Private in the Glider Regiment.
He moved to Addingham in 1990, after living in Ilkley for some time, while working for the Royal Mail delivering post in both places.

George Houston
Born in Scotland, George enlisted in the RAF in 1941, aged 18, and trained as an Air Gunner in Bomber Command. Flying dual, solo, cross country, bombing, low flying, fighter affiliation and air-sea rescue flights. He joined 138 Squadron, Special Operations Executive, at RAF Tempsford, Bedfordshire, in November 1943. His active duty started in January 1944 and, over the next six months, he flew regular missions to France and Belgium and, occasionally, to Norway and Holland. He operated out of bases in Norfolk and Suffolk.

Two more adventures

On 2 June 1944, the week of D-Day, his plane (Halifax LL289, 'P' for Peter) was on a mission ('Percy 7') to drop field supplies to the French resistance, as part of wider Special Operations Executive activity. It was a moonlit night and they flew at an altitude of only 500 to 700 feet (150 to 200 metres)over France even though a Halifax was 30 metres long, weighed 30 tons and was hard to manoeuvre.

It was shot down at Longue, near the River Loire, by a German 88mm gun. The people of Longue thought the Halifax was part of the bombing raid at Saumur and some even believed it was returning from a bombing raid over Italy! It has never been made clear what the final destination of the plane was on its SOE mission: Vercors? Limoges? Only the pilot and navigator knew the destination because of safety and security reasons. Three crew died and were buried in Longue cemetery. Another member of the crew was badly burned and George, having been ejected from the plane, was wounded, but walking. He was soon caught by the Germans, sheltering in a farmhouse owned by Madame Robineau. He was taken to Paris for interrogation and then imprisoned, bizarrely, in Buchenwald concentration camp before being moved, to Stalag Luft 3 at Sagan in Poland, for the rest of the war.
A monument was unveiled on the crash site in 1998.

Support was regularly forthcoming for the brave resistance fighters helping the French people under the yoke of German occupation. Two types of SOE operation existed: air drops of arms, munitions, and food and pick up missions involving parachuting in the agents and helping them, later, to leave France.

George came to live in Addingham, from Bognor Regis, in September 1976 while working for General Electric. In the early eighties, he spent three years in Oman working for the Sultan's Air Force. He died in 2012.

Chapter 5
Plane crashes near Addingham during WW2

The sound of planes, especially during the night, always caused concern, and it was a relief to hear the steady 'All Clear' siren after a wailing 'Warning' siren had sounded.

It was necessary, of course, for our own RAF to train their pilots and crews for both day and night navigation exercises. During the war, on the hills above Addingham, four plane crashes occurred during training exercises, with many casualties.

Here are the details of these four crashes:

(1) Cocking End 1941?

Phyllis Robinson remembers a fighter plane coming down in the Cocking (Cocken) End Wood near Cocking Lane. The date, she said, was the 16th April (it was the Birthday of the brother of her husband Derek) and the year 1941?

The local farmers came to surround the pilot, who came down on a parachute, thinking he was a German. However, they soon realised that he was a British pilot and the plane was a Spitfire!

(2) Windgate Nick, Addingham High Moor, 1943

On March 23rd, 1943, at about 9pm, an RAF Mark 11 de Haviland Mosquito aircraft of 25 Squadron, RAF Church Fenton, crashed into the hillside near

Windgate Nick on Addingham High Moor. The aircraft somersaulted over the moorland ridge, finally coming to rest against the stone wall which divided a field and White Crag plantation. Both crew members were killed:
Sgt. John Hudson Staples – Pilot, and **Sgt. Ralph Ernest Andrews - Navigator**.

The aircraft was returning from RAF Coltishall in Norfolk to its base at RAF Church Fenton near York. From local reports, the aircraft had circled and was thought to be searching for recognisable landmarks. Landowner and farmer Alan Fothergill was aged 9 at the time the plane crashed on his father's land. He was in bed and could hear the aircraft circling above the farm, followed by a very loud explosion, which made his bedroom door blow open. His first thoughts were that the Germans were invading but then he heard the neighbours come to bring news of the crash. Next morning, the moor was still on fire and the sound of exploding ammunition could still be heard. Most of the wreckage of the wooden built plane was burnt on site.

Memorial Stone at Windgate Nick, High Moor

(3) Long Ridge, Ilkley Moor, 1944

On 31st January 1944 the crew of a MkV Handley page bomber, based at RAF Dishforth near Ripon, took off to undertake a cross-country night navigation exercise. Some time into the flight, and about 40 miles south of its intended course, the aircraft was flying in low cloud and mist over the Ilkley Moor and Addingham Moorside area. It crashed into the moorland at Long Ridge at around 5.30pm and caught fire. Of the seven-man crew, six were members of the Royal Canadian Air Force and were killed in the crash. The seventh member of the crew, **Flight Engineer Felix Bryne, RAF**, survived the crash and local people

The memorial Stone at the crash site at Long Ridge, Ilkley Moor

who made their way to the crash site found him and attempted to save his life. They carried him down off the moor on a gate and he was taken to High Royds Hospital in Menston but sadly died soon afterwards.

Phyllis Robinson (who lived on The Moorside) remembers hearing the plane coming up the valley, making a heavy droning noise, and when it came out of the mist she saw it trying to turn up over the side of the moor but she knew it would never make it. Her father went to help at the crash and she said he seemed to be away for a long time. When he eventually returned home it was with sad news about the casualties. It was thought that the aircraft descended through low cloud to find navigational landmarks to help locate RAF Yeadon Aerodrome (now Leeds Bradford Airport).

All the Canadian crew members are buried at Stonefall Cemetery Harrogate. The crew were:
P/O Donald George McLeod RCAF – Pilot
Sgt Felix Bryne RAF – Flight Engineer
W/O Lewis Riggs RCAF – Navigator
Sgt Robert Henry Rahn RCAF – Bomb Aimer
W/O William George King RCAF – Wireless Operator/Air Gunner
Sgt George Martin RCAF – Air Gunner
Sgt Albert Lorne Mullen RCAF – Air Gunner

(4) Beamsley Beacon, 1945

On the morning of 5th November 1945, the crew of a Lancaster bomber was tasked with a cross-country training flight, but the details of the flight are vague.

After take-off, the flight took them south from RAF Leeming in North Yorkshire, and, on their return north, they were met with poor weather to the southwest of the county. On board were at least six regular aircrew of the Royal Canadian Air Force and two ground crew, who were taken up for a flight. The training flight was all but completed and, in all probability, they would only have been in England for a few more weeks before returning home to Canada. The conditions in the Pennines in the mid-morning of this day was described as poor, with mist and low cloud covering the areas of high ground. The aircraft flew on into the low cloud and the crew soon became lost. They tried to radio for assistance but no reply came and the navigator was struggling to work out their position whilst flying in cloud. The only way to try and find out where they were was to descend and hope they could get a visual fix on the ground. This was against flying regulations but many aircraft flew into high ground during the war doing such actions. Unknown to them, high ground lay in front and the aircraft descended below the level of what was the highest hill in its path: Beamsley Beacon. The aircraft struck the southern side of the Beacon, just some fifty feet from the summit, at

11.56am, disintegrated on impact and caught fire. Four of the eight crew were killed on impact.

Trish Gill of Bark Lane reports: *'When the Canadian plane crashed on the Beacon, my late father-in-law, Thomas Briggs Gill, was parked on Nesfield Road with his daughter Ann, having a break from delivering milk. They heard the plane coming over, obviously in distress.*

A Canadian survivor, Joseph Patrick Ballenger (the least seriously injured of the four survivors) managed to find his way to the Pullans' farm (Black Hill Farm, Langbar) from where he was shown the way to Black Foss Farm, (the Gills'), as they had a public telephone in the entrance. Alan (the Gills' oldest son) then went back with him to the site of the crash.

After spending a night or two in Coronation Hospital, Ilkley, with head injuries and suffering from severe shock, he called back at the farm to say thank you, and was invited in to share supper with them'.

The aircraft was also heard to fly over the area by other people on the ground and, upon hearing the crash, many of them made their way up to the crash site, which took some locating in the thick mist. The remains of the aircraft were eventually found and the other three survivors were taken down to waiting ambulances and then on to High Royds Hospital in Menston where, it is believed, they all recovered.

Those killed were:-
Pilot F/O Walter Fred Conley RCAF
Flight Engineer-F/Sgt. Arnold Emerson Stinson RCAF
Bomb Aimer – F/O Wallace Ewing Lang RCAF
Passenger Cpl William John Ellis RCAF
The survivors were:-
Navigator F/O Alan Price Coleman RCAF
Flight Engineer F/Sgt. Francis John Moran RCAF
LAC Reginald Henderson RCAF
Wireless Operator/Air Gunner – Sgt. Joseph Patrick Belanger RCAF

Arnold Stinson had flown to Berlin in late October 1945 where he, and his crew, had spent a few days before returning to base. Frank Moran died in 1968 in an accident when his snowmobile went through the ice on a lake in Ontario which he was crossing at night.

Much of what was found at the crash site was buried by the clear-up party after the crash. Now the only wreckage is in small handheld pieces. In 2006 one large pit was uncovered at the crash site and the contents picked over. The aluminium has been badly oxidised but some harder metallic parts survived in reasonable condition. Many found at the front end of the plane, including items from the flight engineers panel, were alongside remains of a Dalton computer, harness buckles, and a monkey wrench.

Plane crashes near Addingham

*Crash site memorial plaque (lower) for Lancaster RA 571, on Beamsley Beacon
(A memorial plaque was finally erected on the site in November 2015 to
remember both victims and survivors.)*

Chapter 6
In Memoriam

The authors hope that this book will help to ensure that all those involved in the Second World War, whether as servicemen or civilians, will be remembered by future generations for the great debt that we owe them.

In addition, there are two stone-built memorials in the village: The Memorial Hall and the War Memorial itself. Both are notable for being places of recreation as well as remembrance.

The Memorial Hall

Mention has been made above of the work of the Addingham Women's Knitting Circle who worked tirelessly to make 'comforts' for the servicemen from the village, and elsewhere, serving at home or abroad.

During the war ladies across the country set up knitting circles, with the reminder that 'if you can knit – you can do your bit', and they knitted for the Army, Navy, Air Force & ARP workers. Sirdar Wool Co. produced wool dyed in service colours – khaki, navy blue, air force blue & grey.

The Women's Knitting Circle in Addingham (shown overleaf in 1942) met regularly at the Conservative Club. They were a very committed group and

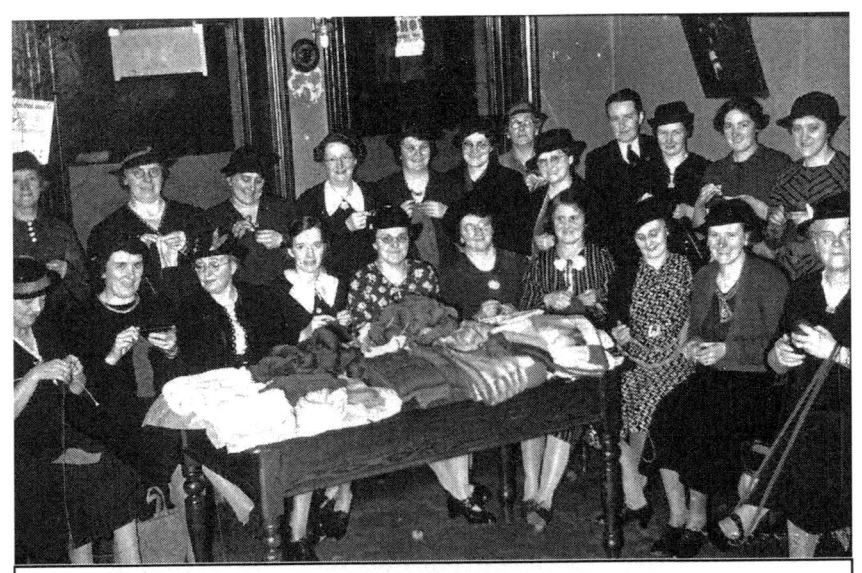

LADIES KNITTING CIRCLE

Back, L to R: Miss Dorothy Ashton, Mrs Ada Hudson, Mrs Cis Hudson, Mrs Minnie Holmes, Mrs Nellie Adams, ??, Miss Brear, Mrs Joseph Brear, Miss Hilda Holmes, Mrs Marion Garforth, Mrs Freda Hood, Mrs Maggie Ashton.
Front Row, L to R: Mrs Adams, Mrs Ellen Lumley, Mrs Ted Holmes, Mrs Jenny Cockshott, Mrs Railton, Mrs Mathews, Mrs Sarah Wilkinson, Mrs Molly Holmes, Mrs Maud Horton, Mrs Mitchell?

Photo: Hilda Holmes, Names: Phyllis Robinson

as a result of the efforts over 500 articles were knitted, with every member of His Majesty's forces from Addingham being supplied with a pullover, scarf, balaclava, two or three pairs of socks and gloves/mittens.

Even Russians on the Eastern front benefitted from their knitting and, at the same time, they were aiming to raise money for a memorial to the men and women of Addingham who had sacrificed so much for their homes and country. In 1946 they had £1,000 invested and a public meeting resolved that the memorial should take the form of a village hall. An elected committee was formed and over the next 12 years raised money by whist drives, dances, children's days etc. which raised the sum £3,790. The Primitive Methodist Chapel had closed in about 1955 and was offered, for £1,000. This was ideal and the generous offer was accepted. However, much more money was needed to pay for the conversion into The Memorial Hall.

Twenty years later a large legacy came to Ilkley and Addingham from James Clarke and his sister Sarah Foley, who had lived in Addingham and Ilkley. At the time there was a debt on the Memorial Hall, which had been enlarged and improved. Money was contributed from the Clark-Foley bequest to wipe out the debt and one of the rooms in the hall was named 'The Clark-Foley Room'.

(from *Addingham from Brigantes to Bypass* by Kate Mason)

Converting a chapel to a much-needed village hall *(above, drawn by Bill Pates in 1993)* was a fine tribute to the young men who gave their lives during the war, ideally placed next to the War Memorial. Thanks to the efforts of local groups and individuals that made this possible, the Memorial Hall continues to provide the village with a popular meeting and social place for present and future generations.

The War Memorial (see overleaf)

The land for the War Memorial and what is now known as Memorial Close, which stands next to the Memorial Hall, was given to the village by the First Lord Masham (mill owner Samuel Cunliffe-Lister) after the First World War, with a plaque listing the many names of the Addingham men lost in that conflict. After WW2, a lower panel was engraved with the, thankfully, many fewer names of those who didn't return from the 1939-45 war.

The Memorial building is dual purpose in that it also houses the Bowls Club pavilion and, originally, also had public toilets at the ends.

The Addingham War Memorial

The Fallen

We end with a moving poem which was written by Laurence Binyon in 1914 and first published in The Times newspaper on 21st September that year, a few weeks after the outbreak of the First World War.

Laurence said, in 1939, that the four lines of the fourth stanza came to him first. These words have become famous having been adopted by the Royal British Legion as an exhortation for Ceremonies of Remembrance to commemorate fallen servicemen and women.

Laurence Binyon was too old to enlist in the military forces but he went to work for the Red Cross as a medical orderly, in 1916. He lost several friends, and his brother-in-law, in the war.

In Memoriam

THE FALLEN

With proud thanksgiving, a mother for her children,
England mourns for her dead across the sea.
Flesh of her flesh they were, spirit of her spirit,
Fallen in the cause of the free.

Solemn the drums thrill, Death august and royal
Sings sorrow up into immortal spheres.
There is music in the midst of desolation
And a glory that shines upon our tears.

They went with songs to the battle, they were young,
Straight of limb, true of eye, steady and aglow.
They were staunch to the end against odds uncounted,
They fell with their faces to the foe.

They shall grow not old, as we that are left grow old:
Age shall not weary them, nor the years condemn.
At the going down of the sun and in the morning
We will remember them.

They mingle not with their laughing comrades again,
They sit no more at familiar tables of home;
They have no lot in our labour of the day-time;
They sleep beyond England's foam.

But where our desires are and our hopes profound,
Felt as a well-spring that is hidden from sight,
To the innermost heart of their own land they are known
As the stars are known to the Night

As the stars that shall be bright when we are dust,
Moving in marches upon the heavenly plain.
As the stars that are starry in the time of our darkness,
To the end, to the end they remain.

Laurence Binyon, 1869 – 1943

About the authors

Beryl Falkingham (née Turnpenny)
Beryl was born and lived in Addingham until after she was married, and then moved to Ilkley with her husband Roy.

She was not quite five years old when her father Ernest Turnpenny died a POW. Her mother obtained news that Ernest was missing, and then a POW, but it was not until the end of the war that she received the news that Ernest had died in November 1942. Beryl was then nearly eight and remembers her Mother receiving the letter with the devastating news.

The last picture of Beryl with her father

Richard Thackrah
Richard has been a resident in the Ilkley district for two spells over the past, nearly seven, decades: firstly in Ben Rhydding and, since 2011, in Addingham. He gained degrees in Geography, History and Education and has taught in primary, secondary and tertiary education. He has written a variety of books including 'A Guide to Ilkley' and 'Victorian Yorkshire', and has completed a major project about an 'Ilkley Timeline 1868 to 2016', concentrating, especially, in a series of booklets and on-line books about Ilkley between 1914 and 1946.

Don Barrett (Editor)
Don was born brought up in Cambridge before moving to Luton to work as a metallurgist in the motor industry. He moved to Addingham in 1995, with his wife Lesley, and has since been active in the Addingham Civic Society and Garden Friends, running the village website (www.addingham.info), and in the production of books about the village.

Other books from Addingham Civic Society:

'Addingham – From Brigantes to Bypass'(1996)
A definitive history of the village, by local historian, the late Kate Mason

'Addingham Houses 1750 – 1850' by Arnold Pacey (2014)
Before 1750 Addingham was a small farming community, but during the next 100 years the village was transformed by the coming of the textile industry and the construction of substantial mills and related enterprises. This book describes the houses built, and who built them, during this period.

'William 'Bill' Bradley, Addingham's Most Inventive Engineer' (2016) by Don Barrett & Ian Crawshaw
This book describes the life of William Bradley from his birth in 1885 to his death at the great age of 98.
Starting as a vehicle repair and servicing mechanic he was also a motorcycle trials rider who designed and built remarkable bikes and he later became a manufacturer of innovative textile industry equipment.

'We Who Served..., Stories of Addingham and The Great War, 1914-1918' by Catherine Snape (2015)
From Addingham, a close-knit village of millworkers and farmers, with a population of less than 2,000, over 400 men marched off to fight in the 1914-1918 war. This book describes the experiences of those men and the families they left behind.

'Main Street Memories, Living and Shopping in 1940s Addingham' by Don Barrett, Beryl Falkingham & Gloria Stitt (2015)
Present day Addingham is very different to what it was during the Second World War and the 1950s.
This book describes the everyday life of two young girls growing up on Main Street during the war and an imaginary shopping trip along Main Street.

(Available from the society – email: info@addinghamcivicsociety.co.uk)

Printed in Great Britain
by Amazon